THE COLLECTED POEMS OF

Lorenzo Thomas

WESLEYAN POETRY

THE COLLECTED POEMS OF Lorenzo Thomas

Edited by ALDON LYNN NIELSEN

and LAURA VRANA

WESLEYAN UNIVERSITY PRESS Middletown, Connecticut

Wesleyan University Press
Middletown CT 06459
www.wesleyan.edu/wespress

Manufactured in the United States of America
Designed by Richard Hendel
Typeset in Miller and TheSerif by Tseng Information Systems, Inc.

Cover art: John Biggers, "Four Sisters" (1986).
Collection of the Hampton University Museum, Hampton, Virginia.
Used with permission.

Library of Congress Cataloging-in-Publication Data
NAMES: Thomas, Lorenzo, 1944–2005, author. | Nielsen, Aldon Lynn, editor. | Vrana, Laura, editor.
TITLE: The collected poems of Lorenzo Thomas / edited by Aldon Lynn Nielsen and Laura Vrana.
OTHER TITLES: Poems
DESCRIPTION: Middletown, Connecticut : Wesleyan University Press, [2019] | Series: Wesleyan poetry | Summary: "Lorenzo Thomas's Collected Poems is a thorough retrospective of the work of a poet of the Black Arts Movement in the United States in the 20th century. Often engaged with political and social upheavals, for example the civil rights movement and Vietnam War, Thomas uses formal experimentation and elements of music and pop culture to reflect upon the transforming experience of being an 'American.'"— Provided by publisher.
IDENTIFIERS: LCCN 2019030467 (print) | LCCN 2019030468 (ebook) | ISBN 9780819578983 (cloth) | ISBN 9780819578990 (paperback) | ISBN 9780819579003 (ebook)
CLASSIFICATION: LCC PS3570.H568 2019 (print) | LCC PS3570 (ebook) | DDC 811/.54—dc23
LC record available at https://lccn.loc.gov/2019030467
LC ebook record available at https://lccn.loc.gov/2019030468

5 4 3 2 1

CONTENTS

PREFACE

Laura Vrana

In his indispensable study *Extraordinary Measures: Afrocentric Modernism and Twentieth-Century American Poetry* (2000), Lorenzo Thomas astutely observed: "The creative activity of African American writers, of course, also paralleled, influenced, and responded to social and artistic developments in the national 'mainstream' culture. This fact [is] largely ignored in 'standard' American literary history." The accuracy of this sentiment is reinforced by the tragic—if predictable—neglect to which it was subsequently subjected by that "standard" literary history. Yet those interested in American poetry writ large and African American literature across genres must attend to Thomas's view, as well as to his oeuvre of work both critical and creative, which has been undervalued for several linked reasons.

First has been the inaccessibility of much of Thomas's poetry in widely available editions, due to the ephemeral means by which he often disseminated it; this collection gestures toward filling that lacuna, though this same ephemerality has regrettably made it impossible to be as comprehensive as might hopefully be attainable in the future. This impossibility points to the second problem preventing full recognition of Thomas's integral role in American and African American literature: his inclination toward experimenting with myriad aesthetics in modes both serious and light-hearted. Like several others who have had the good fortune to become better known, notably Harryette Mullen, who cites him as a key influence, Thomas's refusal to remain within the traditional boundaries erected around African American literary aesthetics often took the form of linguistic and surrealist innovation, inspired by visual artists, writers, and musicians ranging from Robert Johnson and Lightning Hopkins to Aimé Césaire and John Ashbery. Thirdly, Thomas's defiance of geographical and institutional norms left him susceptible to exclusion from subsequent scholarly evaluations of the multiple communities with which he claimed affiliation throughout his career, such as the New York School—with which he was tied via the "Tulsa Group" through Ron Padgett's *White Dove Review* and Ted Berrigan's *C Magazine*—and the Umbra collective. His move to Texas in 1973 and his two-decade career at the University of Houston–Downtown positioned him at the vanguard of dramatic changes in institutional relationships with black writers.

Thomas served as a key connecting force himself, sharing little-known literary and musical artifacts and speaking across the country until his death in 2005. Even as a teen he had performed this role, editing a little magazine, *Lost World*, a 1961 copy of which contains one of his early verses, included here. In an interview with Hermine Pinson published in 1999 in *Callaloo*, he described this role:

> If African-American culture is really going to be properly appreciated, I think what has to happen is that we have to have institutions that we can nurture into longevity even if we know that a half century from now they might be doing something quite different than you and I and today's contributors can even imagine. That's the purpose of having an institution. They will carry on some of our dreams and needs, right? And they should also be constructed in such a way that they will be responsive to a future that we might not even be able to foresee.

It is in this capacity as a preserver of black culture, and through his contributions to documenting a literary history that he was more integral to creating than has been acknowledged, that Thomas's work lives on most directly. Yet his unique poetic style renders another unsung contribution, essential to ongoing scholarly efforts to expand the aesthetic and topical boundaries of the African American literary canon. With the publication of several collections and numerous more ephemeral works over five decades, alongside major essays and studies that helped to shape black literary study, Thomas's works affected American poetry and African American literature from the Black Arts Movement through the contemporary era.

Born in 1944 in the Republic of Panama to politically conscious parents who viewed their world through the lens of pan-African global identity, Thomas would carry throughout his life an unshakably Afrocentric, transnational view of the black experience that never altered even as social contexts shifted. This birthplace meant that Spanish was Thomas's first language and English his second, birthing a skepticism about the supposedly self-evident nature of linguistic structures, semantic rules, and grammatical logics that shaped his playfully experimental and pun-laden approach to poetry. Like Mullen, he occasionally intersperses multilingualisms in a casual manner that still registers as disruptive to some; yet earlier twentieth-century movements that inspired Thomas, including

Negritude, displayed similar transnational and multilingual impulses. Thomas pointed out in a 1981 *Callaloo* interview with Charles Rowell that "If you read the African writers who write in Portuguese, you'll find that they were inspired by Countee Cullen and Langston Hughes.... Hughes was inspirational in Portuguese-speaking Africa and in French-speaking Africa; he was a wonder in Central and South America, where many proclaimed him as the voice of the people, someone to emulate."

Thomas's poem "Robert Williams, Exiled in Cuba" opens by addressing two Cuban artists, poet Nicolás Guillén and visual artist Wilfredo Lam, with a diasporic intimacy that asserts a global and Afrocentric view of blackness. He asks Williams to "[l]ook in the streets / for a dark boy ... / find him and say, 'Lorenzo's / in New York this winter and, you know, he's black too.' // Lorenzo, born in Panama, could look from / his playpen, see the Canal Zone, the stars & stripes. / Could see Uncle Sam's guns aimed at the nazi [*sic*]. / Lorenzo, flying to the states in '47, / Stopped over in Havana one hour, remembers little." The memory detailed runs deeper than one individual's, illustrating Thomas's lifelong commitment to an intellectual and artistic exploration of the worldwide reach of American militaristic imperialism and, simultaneously, the empowering possibility of global black identification. The depth of this commitment transcended biographical circumstances and location, following Thomas and shaping his artistic and critical output throughout his career even though, as the poem narrates, he left Panama at a young age.

Raised in the Bronx and Queens after the international flight imagined in his poem, Thomas earned a B.A. in English Literature from Queens College and began graduate work toward an M.L.S. from the Pratt Institute. While at Queens College, he also joined what would become one of the earliest and most pivotal organizations of the Black Arts Movement: the Umbra Workshop, founded in 1962. During this period, Thomas was influenced by older Umbra artists including Ishmael Reed and Archie Shepp: the multi-genre works produced by such participants as musician-writer Shepp and writer and visual artist Askia M. Touré (then known as Roland Snellings) also affected Thomas's work long-term, encouraging him to incorporate art (often by his brother Cecilio, a commercial artist and book designer) and innovative symbols into his texts, to become a powerful performer of his own work before all types of audiences, and to rely on music as a primary source of inspiration. Thomas was one of the youngest members of Umbra, and his essays and interviews prove an essential source for writing its history; nevertheless, he was too often omitted from early narratives of the workshop, since he became partly disassociated from it before its later controversies.

For in 1968, during the Vietnam War, like other black poets such as Yusef Komunyakaa, Thomas entered the military, serving four years of Navy duty that included education in the Vietnamese language. That was the same year Larry Neal and Amiri Baraka edited and published the influential *Black Fire*, key anthology of the Black Arts Movement, which included Thomas's work. Thomas's exposure to other languages and his military experience resonate throughout his mature verse. Unlike Baraka, Thomas was discharged honorably in 1972; he moved the next year to Houston, where he would make his home intermittently for the rest of his life.

This dislocation might seem an odd move at the height of the Black Arts Movement, which critics tend to view as centered in urban hubs on either coast. But highlighting Thomas's story furthers recent efforts to illuminate the geographical diversity and divergences of the movement's practitioners beyond those obvious poles, as he articulated in the 1981 interview with Rowell: "[t]he Black Arts Movement of the Sixties was never very far from the South." Mullen has called Thomas "one of the messengers who brought the Black Arts movement below the Mason Dixon Line" (see the essay "All Silence Says Music Will Follow: Listening to Lorenzo Thomas," in her book *The Cracks Between What We Are and What We Are Supposed to Be*). We might even view him as having been ahead of his time, for the move was precipitated by accepting a position as writer-in-residence at Texas Southern University; among the first black writers to work in public schools in this capacity, he then filled the same role at Florida A&M University and for the states of Arkansas and Oklahoma. While black writers inhabiting such positions has since become common, this trend was just beginning in the early 1970s, when Black Studies programs and departments were first being established.

Like better-known Black Arts Movement practitioners, Thomas remained devoted to working in his community alongside these university spaces. He helped to edit the arts journal *Roots* out of the Black Arts Center in Houston, where he also taught writing workshops, another demonstration of his role in cementing the cultural centrality of black artists and writing a history in progress. He became active with the Texas Commission of Arts and Humanities and served on the board of directors of the Coordinating Council of Literary Magazines. Further, he organized the Juneteenth Blues Festival in Houston and other cities, directed the Cultural Enrichment Center at the University of Houston–Downtown, and reviewed books for the *Houston Chronicle* for many years. He won a National Endowment for the Arts Creative Writing Fellowship in 1983 and the Houston Festival Foundation Award in 1984. On a panel for a 2002 American Studies Association conference, Maria Damon argues that in Thomas's work

> Afrocentric poetry is historiography, and Afrocentric literary historiography is a form of *social* witnessing. . . . to write the extraordinary linear measures of poetry is to link one's own survival to that of one's community. To write history through poetry and a poetic historiography is to knit oneself even more closely to community. Healing the split between history and poetry, literary history, itself a poetics, can be a way of situating poetic practice in a social context—one's own. By looking at Lorenzo Thomas's literary historiography, we get a sense of how a poet's rendition of history foregrounds the poetics of community formation and historical transformation.

The history surveyed in Thomas's work ranges from ancient Egypt and Afrocentric cosmological mythologies to contemporary American incursions into Vietnam, extending the legacies of Ishmael Reed's early poetry—which similarly integrated ancient myth and twentieth-century political critique—through the changing contexts of the Civil Rights movement, subsequent neoconservative retrenchments, and twenty-first-century iterations of racial terror.

Thomas's continuing in-between aesthetic positionality—by which his work fit either into no aesthetic school or many, depending on whom you query—resulted in such seeming anomalies as his name being proposed as the sole potential black contributor to *L=A=N=G=U=A=G=E* magazine in early discussions among Ron Silliman and the editors. Like Baraka (then LeRoi Jones) in Donald Allen's anthology *The New American Poetry* (1960) and later Erica Hunt in Silliman's anthology *In the American Tree* (1986), Thomas ultimately became the only black writer to appear in that publication. At the same time, he was publishing poetry and criticism widely in such venues as *African American Review*, *Ploughshares*, and the *African American Encyclopedia*, focusing on black literature and music with a critical astuteness that culminated in a posthumous collection of essays, *Don't Deny My Name: Words and Music and the Black Intellectual Tradition*. Such rigorous boundary-crossing in terms of publication venues and connections to other writers seems especially unusual when one considers Thomas's indebtedness to an aesthetic of Afro-surrealism, frequently inspired by Cesaire and in tune with black musical innovation in all genres, including (as Mullen has written) "jazz, blues, R&B, rock, reggae, calypso, zydeco, disco, country western, western classical music, and even muzak." But understanding this defiance of boundaries in (literary and musical) aesthetics and in publication is essential to reading Thomas's work, as my co-editor's Introduction details: his artistic statements (several of which are included at the end of this collection) decimate categories. As he articulated in a 2001 interview in *The New Journal*, his poems

> are influenced as much by Frank O'Hara and John Ashbery as by Amiri Baraka and Calvin Hernton.... what I learned from Ashbery reinforced what I learned from Wallace Stevens and both Ashbery and Baraka reinforced what I found interesting about the colloquial language that I found in Langston Hughes and Carl Sandburg. And, of course, it is a fact that Hughes learned something from Sandburg, too. I guess that is how poetic influence connects you to a tradition. But in this sense I am not suggesting that tradition is a readymade thing.

Indeed, Thomas was always engaged as much in making traditions as he was in suggesting their preexistence, though—as with his critical assertions—those intersecting influences in his work have often been ignored. The resulting neglect of the range of poetic texts Thomas produced, even including a 1997 bilingual German edition of his poems, began to be rectified near the end of his life. His final collection of poetry, *Dancing on Main Street* (2004), featured on its cover praise from Ashbery: "Lorenzo Thomas's poems have a graceful New York School nonchalance that can swiftly become a hard and cutting edge when he writes of the African American experience, especially in his adopted home of Texas. 'This useless clairvoyance / is embarrassing,' he confides. Yet Thomas's brand of clairvoyance is not only useful, but beautiful." That implied divide between "New York School nonchalance" and the "African American experience" rarely plays out in the poetry, which interweaves so many supposedly disparate locations and experiences. Like Mullen, Thomas cleverly "puts the wit back into witness" (as Maria Damon said, quoted by Kalamu ya Salaam), satirically critiquing in often amusing verses Western imperialism, reliance on technology, and understandings of science as irreconcilable with spirituality.

Indeed, Thomas's clairvoyant ability to foresee our moment of black poetics breaking down the boundaries that have attempted to delimit its subjects and forms should render him of special interest to anyone entranced by the recent flourishing of black poets' work. He asserted in the 2001 *New Journal* interview that "a great deal of poetry" seems "to resemble the mental work that occupies us when we are in a condition somewhere between sleep and waking. It has a quality of almost obsessive attention to detail." This evocation of a state halfway between sleeping and waking brings to mind both the surrealist and ancient forms of imagery of which Thomas was fond—and the ghastly realism with which he concisely, comically rips away the veil on American war crimes and the modes of thinking that prop up its methods of domination. In this, his work resembles Reed's and Baraka's. But in other ineffable ways, Thomas's poetry resembles no one else's work at all, the contributions of a singular voice whose unification of seemingly distinct interests helps us to rethink what we believe we know of American poetry and African American literature.

INTRODUCTION

Aldon Lynn Nielsen

> *"If everybody had an ocean ..."*
> *—Brian Wilson*
>
> *"And the orders came down*
> *As your prophets demanded. Strange FM stations*
> *And astrological phone calls hastened to soothe you."*
> *—Lorenzo Thomas*

Admittedly an odd place to begin: mid-1960s, California's white children with their endless summer surfing safari; perhaps not the anticipated opening onto the work of an artist who came of age as a publishing poet at the height of the Black Arts Movement, one of those "Umbra Alums" Harryette Mullen commemorates in her writing. Still, if, as Brian Wilson and the Beach Boys imagined, everybody had an ocean across the U.S.A., then Manhattan and Manhattan Beach might each take a different view of the interior, and that view might well resemble the collaged bacchanal of cleansing and consumption offered up by Cess Thomas in the cover art to Lorenzo Thomas's 1981 collection *The Bathers*, which included earlier works,. Or, turning the page, it could look much like the baptism of Birmingham, that Alabama city that liked to call itself "A good place to raise a boy," the "magic city" that mounted a dogged attack upon its own citizenry in an effort to drown out, as Thomas writes, those "infinite legions of us. Those who toil." Still again, if everybody had an ocean we might gather together on the shore depicted on the cover of 1972's *Fit Music* and wonder what rough beast, its hour come round again, trumpets its resurrection from the foam.

Which should remind us that there were already other beach boys:

> They were all on the beach, and there were many others besides them—white men, brown men, black men, Finns, Poles, Italians, Slavs, Maltese, Indians, Negroids, African Negroes—deportées from America for violation of the United States immigration laws ...

This surely is a census of the infinite legions of us, of those who toil, yet it is just as surely not the scene depicted in all those Beach Party movies of the '60s, in which Frankie and Annette's close personal friends, Stevie Wonder and the Supremes, would drop by to knock out a tune or two of fit music for the gathered bleached tribes, but who were never to intrude further into the plot lines and lives of America's white children. Rather, these were the beach boys of Claude McKay's *Banjo*, circa 1929 on the dock of the bay, in Marseilles. If everybody had an ocean, and if that ocean were not quite as segregated as the cinematic sea offered up by Hollywood, then Annette Funicello and Lincoln Agrippa Daily, known among the beach boys as Banjo, might Twist together in the daily rushes.

Brian Wilson once explained to an interviewer from *Time* magazine: "We're not colored; we're white. And we sing white." The real story was, as it always is in America's racial cosmology, considerably more complicated than the Beach Boys allowed. Lorenzo Thomas would have recognized that on first hearing. "Surfin' U.S.A." had as co-author none other than Chuck Berry, whose melody, blues progression, patented guitar licks, and even idealistic, adolescent longing are at the core of what Brian Wilson made from the materials of Berry's composition "Sweet Little Sixteen." Berry and the Beach Boys, too, shared a common shore of enunciation. The hard "R" sounds and wide-open vowels of Brian Wilson's plain statement resemble nothing so much as the dialect of the plains, the natural affect of Missourians like Melvin B. Tolson and Chuck Berry. (It's a sound that marks the Beach Boys apart from the Okie-inflected pronunciation of so many of their neighbors, not to mention the Armenian strains of contemporaries of theirs such as Cher.) This, unlike the musical appropriations, was not a matter of conscious mimicry, the sort of thing that explains why so many fifteen-year-old white boys in Iowa now sound as though they grew up in the Bronx. But it does raise a rather obvious question: When white people say that someone sounds "black," what do they really mean? Brian Wilson says he sings white, and if that means that he sounds a lot like Chuck Berry, then we need to wonder just what is fit music for an America always at war with its own racial present?

Such questions are unavoidable when reading Lorenzo Thomas. How do we account for a poem titled "Negritude" that begins with beach boys:

> They swim they play the surf for pridefulness
> Their slim boards vanity you see them spread over the pages of
> Life . . .

We would have to begin by recollecting that the founding poets of Negritude found themselves far from home, writing from the banks of the Seine in notebooks of a return. We would also have to acknowledge the ambiguous connotations oceans hold for black American poets. Lucille

Clifton remarked to me how long it took her to be able to celebrate the Atlantic, where the traces of Middle Passage still gleam fathoms deep beneath the tempest. She said that she is able to contemplate the Pacific in another way. But there another order of oddity prevails. In Thomas's "Fit Music" we read: "The sun people bleach their hair in the sun // If I mention Isis they ready to fight." The Pacific fronts on Vietnam, which brings Lorenzo Thomas to the central questions posed by "Fit Music." If Ezra Pound's Confucius fits into a poem that Thomas subtitles "California Songs, 1970," we can explain it in part by the Pacific Rim of association. The shores of the Pacific, whose very name disarmingly connotes peace, are shared by Kung, Buddha, and the Beach Boys. James Brown's "Is It Yes Or Is It No," the song seemingly unique among Brown's prodigious output in never having been reissued on a CD compilation, might seem nominally less Pacific in orientation. Still, it too finds its way into the mix alongside Pound and Wilson, as all three were not only part of the soundtrack of Thomas's California dreaming, they were also, as Thomas's note to the poem slyly states, poets to be acknowledged for "their timeliness and aptness of thought." (In those days, it has to be said, James Brown was always right on time.) The *New York Times* advertises itself as the reliable source for all the news that fits. Pound prescribed a poetry as news that stays new. Thomas's poem, like any breathtakingly novel remix, takes as its point of departure all music that is fitting. "Is It Yes Or Is It No" fits in any number of ways. The open-ended question of Brown's title suggests the seriality of Amiri Baraka and the then New Jazz, the compositional techniques that could be taken in hand to great effect by such disparate artists as Ornette Coleman, Charles Olson, and Baraka.

When the poet of "Fit Music" felt the draft, it was decision time, Canada or conscription? "It was time to be going," we read in the "Proem," to "Vancouver," site as it happens of a most famous '60s symposium of the New American Poetries, "or South Viet Nam." "Is It Yes Or Is It No" was released side by side with Brown's string-drenched "It's A Man's Man's Man's World," a song whose instantly recognizable chord patterns formed the basis for Alicia Keys's signature hit "Falling." Though these Brown songs were considerably more gender-troubled than "I'm Black and I'm Proud," they still serve to frame "Fit Music." What's a man to do? Confucius, Thomas recollects with the aid of Pound's troubled translations, "went on plucking the k'in and / Singing the Odes." Yet Pound was a "certified madman," confined at Saint Elizabeth's Hospital by the same state the poet now contemplates from a farther shore.

"Here in beautiful California," he notes, "the surf remembers another form / of revolution." Begin by taking this as literal truth, surf being a gravitational memory of the moon as the globe makes its revolutions. The poet is marking time, recalling songs and "Sending back reports from the beach." It is a curious space to inhabit, westward in anticipation of transhipment to a war in the East. Admonished, as it were, to get ready to get your ass "in gear."

"Little Honda," though still available, occupies a position in the Brian Wilson oeuvre as anomalous as the fate of James Brown's "Is It Yes Or Is It No." It did appear on a Beach Boys album and was released as a single, but most people's memory of the song is of the radio-hit version performed by The Hondells, who also appeared playing the song, of course, in one of those seemingly countless beach party flicks. It is rather as if "Sweet Little Sixteen" were known primarily through the Beach Boys' shadow version. But the fact that there was a hit record titled "Little Honda" at all speaks to the slippery political and historical terrain of Thomas's poem. Only two decades following the Second World War, millions of American teens clasped Japanese-manufactured transistor radios to their ears and tapped their feet to a theme extolling the virtues of a Japanese vehicle. What tenor was being read out of this as troops enplaned again for war in Asia. The opening stanza of the eighth canto of "Fit Music" begins, in Poundian fashion, by incorporating the chorus of "Little Honda:"

First gear it's alright
Second gear. Lean right
Third gear, hang on tight
Faster

But the poet's report from the beach ends on a more ominous note. Where the Walter Cronkite of the time signed off on his daily reports by intoning, "That's the way it is" (this authoritative voice itself the very reason many on the Right to this day hold Cronkite personally responsible for pronouncing the war in Vietnam a losing proposition), Thomas declares, "That is what's happening in the time warp." This is a time warp he shares with all who, like the Canadian "dangling man" of Saul Bellows's novel, await war. Back in the day, no matter our draft number, we greeted one another with a most sincere request for a status report. Asking "What's happening?" of one another had a particular edge at a time when one's fate could so easily change from moment to moment. Brian Wilson's

"First gear, it's alright" was one Zen-like response. More to the point was Stevie Wonder's "Baby, everything is alright, uptight, clean out of sight." Here, in the time warp of our own habitation, as we again wait to find out if we will be at war, our answer is the much attenuated "aiiiggghhhhtt." Wilson's gear-shifting response had existential concision to recommend it; rather like the old joke I first heard from Gil Scott-Heron about the man who jumped off the Empire State Building. As he fell past the open windows of each subsequent floor, the workers inside could hear him saying, "So far, so good." As the '60s became the '70s, the question was how that sense of alrightness was to be asserted against the conjoint madness of war and racism. Thomas offers us his "Proem" to "Fit Music" as a gloss, "Deja vu more or less," and what could be more familiar to us now, as the raptures of rampant globalism give way to the same old saber rattling, than the Proem's beachside second-person address:

> You spent childhood rehearsing the Korean War
> You fucked up in college and picked the wrong major
> And in 66 everyone faked concern for Asia
> It was all more fitting than you thought;
> The staging.

It was Chuck Berry who warned us to look out for the safety belt that wouldn't budge. When the orders reached us in that long, dark staging area of the soul, what was left but to seek fit music? "Without character," Kung cautions in Pound's thirteenth canto, "You will be unable to play on that instrument." Pound or Brown, Beach Boys or Berry, all go to comprise the poet's character as he confronts the calamity not of his own making, as "An ignorance and circumstance // somehow involve [him] / in their fathers' greed."

There is an envoy, a return to California at the end. Thomas's "Envoy" recalls us to its double reading, and the poet, like the reader, has much to answer for:

> How did you like being the envoy of a monstrous epic
> Or saga of Western corruption
> When the white guys blacked their mugs
> Before the ambush, what did you do kid?

What sort of ambush is it when the Beach Boys borrow blackness as a means to be white? What does it mean when bleached boys blacken their faces to attack in the night? Why are they so ready to fight at the mere mention of Isis? What might it mean that this envoy wraps itself around a strand of musical DNA contributed by James Brown?

As it says in the song making me
Suffer was it fun
Making me suffer
Now I want to know

In Thomas's lineation, it is the song that makes him, as well as the song that makes him suffer. (I remember a great song by John Lee Hooker, one of those existential Blues that underscores our basic sense of our condition, titled, "It Serve You Right to Suffer.") One thing the poem intends is a counter narrative.

In the aftermath of withdrawal, a time often marked by a sense of regret and exhaustion, a myth took hold in the American media, a story of returning Vietnam vets being spat upon in the airports of our nation, as though these were filled at the time with impolite, well-traveled Leftists. The fact that not one credible historian has been able to confirm a single instance of this behavior has done little to dislodge the mythology, whose political power is still deployed in contemporary debates over war and patriotism, though, to judge from the malicious treatment of Vietnam vet Max Cleland in his re-election campaign, those who have availed themselves of this mythology are seldom really interested in benefitting any actual veterans. What Thomas's envoy tells us is of an infinitely more disturbing order:

I wanted somebody to stop me at the airport
And ask me all about Vietnam
But nobody asked me

This surely is part of what it means to stand as an envoy of a monstrous epic, to feel oneself an unattended afterthought, to stand on the stage after the song itself is through and ask, "Was it fun / Making me suffer?"

What welcome does greet this envoy is the golden arch of a San Francisco McDonald's:

A beckoning out the cold, windy night
A rainbow promising nothing
And a warning that that nothing
Is serious business

Square business, indeed. It was just a few years earlier that James Baldwin had reminded readers, "God gave Noah the rainbow sign / No more water, the fire next time." Capital, not God, raised the golden arches to heaven, spanning the babel of international consumption. The descending poet knew "That nothing was bringing me back / Back to de Plantation." Home on the plantation people don't ask about Vietnam; they ask, "Did you by lucky chance / Buy a camera a stereo deck." These were the icons of conquest our vets were expected to bring back with them. The golden arches, in their ubiquity, signal something else about being an envoy. The Beach Boys, in the chorus to "Surfin' U.S.A.," mine a mystical paradox: "Inside, Outside U.S.A." The war in Vietnam was about, among other things, what was termed in those days "spheres of influence." A poet who knew enough to come in out of the Cold War would know the difficulty of discerning just where the American sphere begins and ends. Inside, Outside U.S.A.—not your grandfather's double consciousness, as Thomas would observe.

A NOTE ON THE TEXTS

Across a long writing and publishing life marked by experimentation with language and innovation in forms, Lorenzo Thomas was inconsistent in his usage when it came to matters of capitalization and punctuation (for example, his on-again off-again relationship to the lowly period), and he often used non-standard spellings. One has only to compare his poetry to his published prose to see that these were matters of conscious choice, not accidentals. Most of the poems in this edition were published more than once, and so we are able to see when Thomas chose to leave a poem as it was and when he chose to make an alteration. In our effort to honor Thomas's methods of composition and editing, we have chosen as copy text the last version of the poem that appeared under the author's supervision. In a very small number of cases we have made silent corrections to anomalies we were persuaded had not been intentional.

Early Crimes

. . . .

I

The way Egyptians used to sit
she sits
listening to the radio
Glass room trembles,
the people panting to be
average people
nothing to do with her
Sit erect in an ordinary
chair

The way she sat, her hands
pressed together

Monarch

Sunlight come into the dark
garden of the radio's

insatiability   Chew up
our peaceful moments

Flowers,
before the "news"
The 2nd stage etc etc etc

The age we live in doesn't matter

She is not at home

She is somewhere pressed into
stone

Thinking foreign thoughts
to our music

Some mixup, huh

. . . .

II

She is a new cut out

Her white outline exposes the news
broadcasts

Her dissent is like that
of the music

She is an oracle
her existence,

And I am so graceless their prophet
who does not know her

The people the people

She just walk down the street
and expose them

Listens to the radio

It is not 7:30 it is night now

here in New York
City

And now the news

. . . .

III

Sit erect in an ordinary chair

Her hands touching
the water

The "beauty of strength"
and movement,

Most of the people aren't average

They ordinary

The hands put together

Behind the bookcase glass
is a copy of *The Imprisoned*
Splendour

Some others with brown paper covers
Look like they're bound in gold

THE UNNATURAL LIFE

What I am is a man alone
imprisoned in white
—Aimé Césaire

You know, I keep coming back to the Crown
Delicatessen   It reminds me of you
I see your happy face in every blond table, my
Red embarrassed smirk in the edges of beer
Bottles   The irresponsible public hero above
The stainless steel "take out" counter,
My picture is in that cheap frame
And you are that first dollar pasted on the mirror
I have been so busy of late, translating
"Two or Three Chants" by Leopold Senghor and
Thinking about the coming revolution   You know,
Something got on my mind, I had to come back
It is my lucky day   I am in the Crown Delicatessen
And you are not here
The peach tree spreads on the white house
Behind your house   It is a simplified heart sketched
Like a delicate jacket, its nude design
Reflecting the pack of cigarettes in the pocket
The delay of the plunger in the flooded backwater
Kitchen, the hot curses over the idea of "some ale"
And the idea of revolution is also depicted:
The cashier returns and pays for his life
Because everything is going to be everything.
My copy of Muhammed Speaks covers the table and the wind, and
The door hanging open, frightened because I am here
That I might forget these young delusions of love, afraid
As I emerge from my fashionable jacket   my brain turns
Black and hateful   Like a beast, your color rising in my nose
And you are raped and murdered in the usual manner.
The same peach tree in the backyard spreads on the white house
Behind your house   It is a simplified heart,
See the blind aorta sketched over the vacant bedroom windows.
I should never have moved into your neighborhood!

ONE NEVER KNOWS, DO ONE

For you, I wanted to be so fancy ...
I wanted to be into everything, but you understand
That. Everyday you kept telling me
"Stay loose"   Did you know it was a cliché,
Maybe you were carried away, baby
By the deep, lovely fog in my face. I was
So far out   But suddenly, it moves
In on the area about me (what brakes   fens   etc)
Then today I see young Walters on the
Avenue and he is gone Left Bank, the whole bit—
Camera slung over his shoulder, dungaree
Shirt   I was never that far out, only collegiate.
You understand that, and the dark crevices
Burned into my flesh by the clouds.
You will be glad to know that now I am
So much more interested in private life, other
People's too   And there's something else.
You and my mother both, you will be so
Pleased to hear what I have to tell you. I agree with
You now. I really like "Cabin in the Sky"   You'll
Be so glad to know that now I also agree with
Your vision and judgment of my own handsomeness,
That I did not get that process I wanted.

NEGRITUDE

They swim they play the surf for pridefulness
Their slim boards vanity you see them spread over the pages of
Life hostaged
By photographers who talk like hipsters jewish to their very noses
Infatuate beholden to that scrim of glass and light
The manufactured cataracts of defeated capitalism japanese and german
Eastman Kodak a fine and studied blindness
What will our vacation cost I mean in terms of pride
Mornings when I rise riding the long subway all the way uptown
Half asleep crossing the Columbia campus me glowing in Ferris
Booth's high glass
I love a slim black boy. I love you
And come to work in my own inferno 300°F. covered with surfboards
Rushing everyday to make the historic effort
But after three days sweat's no catalyst I fear my cop out's from
Exhaustion energy's decomposition by fahrenheitic half-lives not
arrogance
My father years ago waiting tables in the Tivoli
Won't towel dance the customers to tips runs out screaming Crème
de menthe on rye
Carstairs alamode!
Maybe there never is another job well I'd rather be in alleys & shake
bone dice.
His wife is pregnant in the hospital San Ignaz
Yeah some of that arrogance is me: the bleak edge of the book, notes
On Function
In placid waves of plate glass or my Nikon's eye, mornings when I rise
The spontaneous book notes what a particular girl says I love you. And
I love you
It is a thing apart from everything the people have.

DOMESTIC HORROR

The house is like the venerated tibia, a chink heirloom
Final statement of some long-nailed uncle.
Kitchen bears a constant smell of butter, huge pots of rice cover
the walls
Everywhere things frying in brittle cast-iron skillets.
She stands against the window her profile dark against parhelion
Yellow walls. Yellow walls to drift out of the city like ordinary
clouds made to
Destroy the confines of the room. 14 × 11, designed by a russian cubist.
The walls float high above New York harbor, this house I keep telling you
It's just too damn near the airport. Pan Am hanger in the living room,
a browntoned
Photograph taxis past all day, coldeyed 1920ish *khanyapa*,
Great floppy beige hat and rimless spectacles: that same young woman
of the
Kitchen dressed in a pale, wiser former body. All day they talk, the
lady on the wall
Giving directions: "More flour in that gravy, O my daughter."
Look! Out on the wild streets of the afternoon a palsied mother and
father in slow
Motion. Galloping home, their well-formed daughter all blond curls
clinging
To the father's drunken, twisted back. But they're too ugly for a
poem of this quality.
Wait, who is this dead child bounding through our home, devouring
the furniture?

TOIL

I has taken all that I can stand
And now it is heroism

Someone to tell you my story
The NEWS photographers crowd
Across the lonely Hudson pier
Shouting interviews,

Ta ta. I'm going to swim to Greece
Who am I trying to impress
You burst into tears late!
My lips gargle "Goodbye"
The rosy sunrise envelops me,
My arm hooks into the night

EMBARKATION FOR CYTHERA

And out of the solitude
Voice and soul with selves unite
—C. Okigbo

This color, its pure absence
in other words a space
        some African mothers, children
cupped in their slim arms
They are bending into the sand
and it is their lesson written there.
            A new motif of
                Destruction—
The idea of a written language
            when before,
the words in our
        mouths were enough.
    Not that it takes anything away
from the people we are,
            "Education"
You don't write "corn" if you
        mean okra.
Along Merrick Blvd, standing in front
the dance hall
            it's the same thing, the
    cop in a luminous blue
His badge spreads all over his face,
threatening me. There should be
        someway to get in without paying.
        Rain that falls into the dusty
            life of the people on
the street, it turns into a new language
All the fine mommas walking inside,
getting out of Grand Prixs
    Can hardly read
this paper without stumbling over "embarkation"
What someone has done to us, that
            my words become unintelligible.

It says, do not despise your own
I wonder if they see that,
All those foxes. All of a sudden
I'm so glad I have on my wide
Pants, my 10 dollar banlon shirt
The girls wish I was
inside, too. At least, I think so
This much is understood
I go down to Benson's Burgers
and sit in the parking lot.
Food smell, but I don't have any money
All I have is the blues
and a ticket for someplace called Cythera
a bus outing on Sunday.
Got this magazine telling about the great
new thing going on in Nigeria
and I have my beautiful high
a green alcove of the evening
called "music"
My voice when it is understood,
piped into dancehalls and restaurants by
this very intricate and lovely machine.

THE BLOND SINNER

Should I be handsome vested and wearing the black
Trench coat of another person's sleepiness,
Collar turned up over my chin and impression
Of terrible guilt; that I'm here with you
Beautiful as you are anxious, beside you
Wearing your own impeccable decision to be night
In all its mystery and cigarette smoke radio—

Sitting around listening to the clock and the birds
Who are singing their morning which is my dark
Night except for them   The single machine comp-
Letes my stranger's hours and I awaken "used"

ECONOMICS

The idle boys are waiting in the park
Girls fear but girls fear anything
When they have been told these boys
Aren't thugs, they're charming
Cut outs and smiling locker doors

Open up the minds of the young people
And reveal them as forms of romance
The naked gymnasium stands among simple
Working class houses whose pretense
Is sitting pretty our solidarity our

Sty of stupid rapport, the miniature cheap
Mentalities MADE IN JAPAN caress her
But she longs to wear black serapes
From bleached balconies to give her sign
To the villagers that he is returning
And the weather reports are indecisive

For one half of the body returns as vapor
To the mind the other half as nerves
The words are the business of the dream
And its wisdom is moving so far away
That easy   The street returns us home

Who are thinking of going to Europe
To sit in the classical sunny gardens
Reading newspapers blackened by race
Demonstrations, new chemical states
Rising in the bewildering absence of Europe

I rise now from my vacant chair
Thought depending on application
The room is in favor of longing
A bride illustrating scholarly ideas
Once more apprehends the afternoon

Taking shape in the air over the garden
We hopefully flee to, escaping dark
And unsavory developments in the way
The mind works today forming cabinets
We dumbly put our trust in and sit back

Pleased with this life we living smiling
At how we have apprehended the time itself
How we have put it to work at a profit
How those who can't understand ECONOMICS
Can steal watches to sell in the park

It quiets the mind to think of transactions
Like this   Even the vandals are part
Of the affluence our bodies exercise
And what spirit keeps thanking the heart
For its numerous changes

The book beside you called ECONOMICS
Which will be sold as PASSION FRUIT
In drugstores, bringing back thoughts
Of small consequence   Sitting here
Say in a garden overlooking a river
Watching another toll across the bridge

Constructed (it says here) not to link
The country and the city but instruct
Pilots in handling their other emotions,
To thrill the people who look on it
With the steel web of their thoughts

That suddenly traps the air around them
And in it the insects of destiny they
Soon recognize as themselves   A genus
Of winged creatures expanding as time does
Seeking the profit of secrets of light

HOW CAN I PROVE I AM NOT MODIGLIANI

We are not capable of lasting fault
Our errors change nothing
Our personal conception like
The vain sandals you wear
Cramp you and smell bad in the rain
But no one says nothing about it
And expect no explanation from
The sky, one moon and one star
We go on and make these mistakes

■

Because I have these things to say;
The moon shines down over it and
Miscellaneous references cloudy
The gold star you pin to my shirt
Another dumb mistake without any

Meaning beyond the pink shadow it
Husbands in my saddening thought
That the moon again is some reflection
Of the thing that misleads us,
Which is another stupid mistake

■

Hate to go out on the street you're such
A smarty always coy and disgraceful and
Pointing out events our horoscope misplaces
The girl sitting there with red shoes on
Wearing a flower dress, thumbs past the
Greatest 20th Cent. painters like a snob
She very well could be   Some men like these
Effects in a woman like drinking bad wine
Has a mystique or keeping your overcoat on
In usually placid houses tempting Satan

Listening to music annoyance odors
There is something persistent about you
You are always blaming me for it
How can I prove I am not Modigliani
But simply and trustingly another
Person who falls ill to the breeze
Coming over the marsh to the city
How can I prove that I have no intention
Of asking you to go on a diet or wear
The autumn's foolish clothes, trust
Me there is nothing that far away as
The museum where we chat and pretend

We see each other and our beauty
Exits like summer grass into danger
We may run into people as charming as we are
And start a flame in their heart
Consume their error as judgment
Treat them as lovers yet be unaware
Of seeing in them, not beauty but
That plainness in them makes them lovely
In our eyes they are more beautiful
Than what is truly beautiful and travels
With nothing insignificant as beauty.

GREAT LOVE DUETS

The sensation created by the human voice
Surrounds the bare lightbulb and makes
It a radio bringing down the cultivated
Air of this room and the slum section

Of the city the soul seeks its order
Amid the disorder of tenement streets
So strange that in these poor neighborhoods
So many women named Mimi are singing to him

The voice in the hand of our imprecision
New York language which forms its cold
Beauty around a steel heart like flowers
Crystals. Is it in spite of the Earth's

Heart uh some miracle speaks to the people
Wrapped in the sounds of their hesitation
These are the children of immigrant legends
The art students sit drinking 98¢ chianti

The words? Even a child's grammar cd explain it
To him, although most children wouldn't believe
And seek other justifications in the time literature
Their parents "make believe" and the art students

Who gather at their soda shoppes
And discuss in front the radio
Sonatas they are now so fond of
They play one dull station all

The time it is playing the same pretty
Sonata about a beautiful young girl
Living in sin with a mad violinist
Somewhere in the awful slums of NYC

And of all the people she thought
She would not mind being in love
Only one was not there, who she loved
Thinking won't it be charming when

We decide to draw the purple covers
All the art students were thinking
"She framed me" and they all desire
One who goes up the stairs and stops

By the window in the light of another
Sonata the deep background the backyard
Presents, people sit on their stoops
Drinking from beercans and pleading

"Cut it out" to the voice that insists
On the news

Across from this island of stone
Smoke rising up in the still air

The voice which will recline on the flat air

The heavy barges on the river headed
For Belgium taking the concentration
Of the lazy youngsters sprawled
Derelicts of the sunlight on the

Grassy hillsides. On the graying divan
Lessons in English grammar are inter-
With the languor of a deliberate kind
Of romance with its blue 35mm pictures

Ringing down the curtain on the sonata:

The words? There are no words
Still the singing is heard

Why are we so foolishly engaged   our environs
Why are we allowing crime to insist
On describing our form everything even
Our gray gloves become suspect, even!

Said the students illustrating their English
THE CLAUSE

Let its dreams carry like echoes
Across the distances another song
To seize her in her lovely trance

Another night in New York City it's snowing
And still they insist on studying yoga

Oh wretched one, why have you driven my time
Away into this forest of stone the wind
Laughs at   Oh wretched one you have made
Me the fool of the unfaithful seasons and

This discipline you reveal in my dis-   sd the students.

Where in this street an art student
Is seen with his clumsy portfolio
Lights a du Maurier and meets his
Girl wondering what will the thrill

Be like this time? Another student
Cries "That face, I must paint it"
Somewhere in New York in the snow
The news again challenges our speech

The speech or the voices of our young people
The radio newscast reporting now the mad student
Leaps on the poor girl with his brush and pot
Of paint and paints her face some innocent hue

Dripping on her white somnolent dress
Causing her boyfriend to despise her
Singing that he loved only her guilt
The schizoid art students of Minnesota

Have come to New York City and ruined
Our city what with their crimes of bad
Grammer "farm life" German extraction
The schizoid art students of Minnesota

ENGAGEMENT

Keep your trust with him and do not go near
The dunce of charity who seeks to hold you
By your own want and tells his to physicians
Leaving his gifts a noontide charm of dew
Your hopeful orchard fields darken with fear
Buttoning the shirt we have depraved with flowers
Against the sudden cold rain
We do not see the force that makes us fall
Prey to the whining genius of the dark
Hours stealing our casual garden the march
Of our imagination to the lake and the arc
The light builds there, and we must fall
Victims to the petty erosions of the dark
The picture of the beautiful lake:
The secretive launch pressing our suspect horizon
Someone loves you the green wave you float on
You are our sensuous lady but exceedingly dull
So what will you have now, your dominion
You burn like the moon in the night for what
Trembling leaf in a pond and for whose sake
He would see currency in your lies and mark
The coursing of your blood a plot
Don't you hear what the chariot says
As it crushes the air we are excited
To breathe   Don't you hear teenage songs
From 1956 flowing around your knees like
The surf we remember last summer afternoons
When you press your lips softly on the
Letter you send me or telephone and argue
With me about inconsequential events of
The air, why are you hearing only our voices
Only the signature of the electric space
We confine to chaperone us
The pedestrian bridge over the highway and
The moonlight; auto lights like an electric river

Sound of the wheels like a stagnant pond
Under the evening   under the summer moon
Did you hear the Chinese verses the tires
Were saying, telling you the direction
These words are taking which way over
The strange map of our feelings. Our feelings.
Our feelings. Our feelings   Are we trapped
In the speed of the mind's careless radar
Zone where I am the driver   If I were the driver
The airy car would run through villages
Through dark and accident and rain
Securing the award of my attentions
To you, which is a prize I wd greedily covet
And drive angrily to win year after year
Don't you hear the proud heart's cylinders
Facetiously singing
The moon is rouge on the horizon's foggy face
To ask her for one dance, the dense
Fog of the 2-step recorded music
Coming to circle the womanly heart
Of the night; goes through his head.
How can it be that he is not the lover
She has sought in her French books
His regard is for her the etiquette of statues
Another time he speaks to her in French
Which is a voice so distant calm and grave
And its inflections darling gauzy Sundays
He invites her into the Bijou's white frame
Where the minutes admire the beautiful fan
And her escort sleeping in the light

THE CONVENTION

The din of your heart on a desolate evening
Across the bleak court your white tears flash
In a soft room. The sharp hands
Replace the garish furniture and
Still I sit here the last image of
Your striking care. The autumn snow
Collects the summer sky's debris and
Still the green stems twine around
Their stake of civilization
The one word it would hurt me to chip
From the glitter in my mouth
Instead of the phone call   this poem
And can't say it. The murkish flood
Idle logic now distilled in your flesh
The silvered tears
Images of our separation
When I remain untrue to
Anything   The desolation
Shimmers in my pleasures
And takes back my thoughts from you
Instead of my raw breath, I give you
Fear drives me back to the convention
My feelings, to have for an afternoon.
Then we understand each other,
All is returned to me   And
Still it resembles the thoughts
Of me you keep in a beautiful
Carton in your room, somewhere
Across the city that now seems
So strange, accepting the convention
We live for but never mention:
You are not free to acknowledge
These terms such is our agreement
Then we understand each other
You got it. Then slowly walk out

The room and out in the gathering
Street. The gold flood of the gut-
Ters sunlight and motor oil
Thinking that what our beauty
Finds in the street's disorder
Can return in the quiet hotel
The conventional neon light making it Spain
Anything else we wd want to believe
Shoddy sense of improvement and
An immaculate joy. Standards
Concerning the function of beauty
And all the love-light shining
In the eyes of a deceased photo

The gone Election Day signs;
Simply to anticipate feelings you had
Already included in your sighs
She offers me the terrain
Of her heart in bondage
I enter and provide its wage
When I sat down at this table
A prophet and now to finish
This ravishing book and have it
Bound in expensive white paper
Filled with the conventional words
Bringing a little strain
Her breath and mine play tag
In lush, bitter arbors
Our wasted hammocks sag
Gladiolas filled with tears
Wrung from the scattered burden
Of trees burnished with rage, our rage
Autumn embroidery in a raw cage
Containing joy, leaking disdain
Holes full of sky in the trees
Her lover crosses his red knees.
Embarrassing.   That's right
She offers me   you offer me a jeweled
Motorcade to trust my heart to

But I am not interested. The one
To whom this heart belongs is she
Who hears it singing everywhere
Conventional as honesty in love is.
Discarding daylight's forgery of
Manners, midnights's emerald stair
Then we understand each other
Except the Africa of her mouth

SONG

You asked me to sing
Then you seemed not
To hear; to have gone out
From the edge of my voice

And I was singing
There I was singing
In a heathen voice
You could not hear
Though you requested

The song—it was for them.
Although they refuse you
And the song I made for you
Tangled in their tongue

They wd mire themselves in the spring
Rains, as I sit here folding and
Unfolding my nose in your gardens

I wouldn't mind it so bad

Each word is cheapened
In the air, sounding like
Language that riots and
Screams in the dark city

Thoughts they requested
Concepts that rule them

Since I can't have you
I will steal what you have

Dracula

DRACULA

Crosses his blond eyes to think of you
Picks up his brown overnight bag and
Runs down the ash covered streets to the station
Scuffles with the ignorant ticket agent
Leaps on the bus as it belches forward
Passengers seeping into the dark
The city is obliged to be dark
And mysteriously desolate under
Ritualized demands of departure
The foolish moon of your care and
Coins filtering through his sheer pockets
A shroud with pockets   cape
His personal state of permanent transit
Covered with decals where he ever mailed
His possessions   This is serious business.
A brand new black greatcoat neatly folded
Over his naked arm the dance of human fluid
"Blood" in more polite times.   The tattoo
Remarkable and genteel,
Pictures of mountains
And soft undistinguished
Rivers in his hand   Across his dry palm
                                        bus ticket dup-
                                            lication designs

The awkward sneer impinging on his nez
                                            This particular
                                                Place
Dracula depicted in venetian half-   light
dissolving boundaries of his presence:

Dracula   your white faces
                            against the night
                        Hair falling back

over your faces

formula STORY

Personal history to that man was particular
Actual form and the descriptive logic of it
The word he thought it was
Was death, was the stiffened sense
O the garments only a sob story
That we could say here was a person
And the person a loss to himself
How strange how strange. The bed-
Room of the most facile delusions

And the clothing edging the plump door
A frighteningly ponderous human body
Suddenly the face of Charles Baudelaire
Crushing on the television screen
Waking the thick solitude of common-
Place individual people.   Confused

Lost.   A man whose heritage and biography was death
He said so

Past back
in the mornings
with your content
to be what person
you are completely

And demanding this song
From me, the personal
History of a single man
Yes, but who are you

■

Start the thing over again:
DRACULA is not a myth but
Just another cheap novel
Written in the boring 18th
19th century made into the
Worst film of 1932 1958 and
Unless we get wise to our-

Selves next year over again
Then what is all this

Dracula is real   Dracula is real!

ESSAY   The demands of the loving human flesh
substance

A man and himself.
European habits

Colorless eyes filling the empty sleeves
Of the earth, another Slavic conception

After we keep on asking,   What is that in the gypsy
language

What is that thing we no longer discover
Effective about our own faces in the glass
Underneath the B♭ chandelier
The final odors of our dinner in person
Shudder in the monotonous drawing room
Still you have nothing else to amuse you

It compels.   It compels
The imprint of his RNA
On physical objects and
Space   he insists on it,
Insists he has been dead
Over 300 years and we
Suggest we believe it
After the trance we put
On our hypothetical
Subconscious mind   Dracula
Dracula is real!   good lord!
How do we understand it
It is life you have founded
Death's mythology on, when

Your substance demands   Get
Out of that umbrella now
Right now.

And now you are brushing yr teeth
With the language, trying to get
The decay out of the classical music
That lurks behind each evident crime

Every clumsy seduction of falseness
And mechanical simpering pride that
Moves like a film across the eyes
Distorting the incredible color of

Summertime on crowded sands
An unashamed obvious bur-
Lesk moving like a sloppy
Sneak thief in the dreams

Floating like sunlight into an awful
America white and unhappy as drawn
by a dull artist who lusts and his
Creations for the darkness of blood

And insane crime.   But it's a crime
What he's doing and beyond statute
THIS IS A WORK OF ART no matter how
Unnecessary it remain to our flesh

■

These last lines of it spoken by the midnight doctor
And left hanging in the flat air over the station
To be snatched by the violent train of his thoughts
Suspended sentences drawing sighs from the placid
Snake tooth mouth of our Dracula.   Changes his form
Assumes an entire jury of peering witnesses walking
Deliberately like negroes on the street,
And then the strict transformation rabble
Screaming and waving pockets torn off

The most respectable fences in the town
A lynch mob.   Simple.   This is nothing
With symbols except the holy mystery of
Our people in this country today.   God
Have charged them with the presence of the unwanted
The necessary black negro   and this is the way
Our people bear their judgment
There is no release in the songs
Their music is dying   They try to steal
Heat for the beautiful instruments again
The black ones learn to play these
Machines but they leave our people screaming
Silence   Nothing happens.   More nothing and
The loss of the land hangs in the air
A rotten rapist.   Stomach full of bloody
Advertising.   Sculpture or is it dance
The hanging orchards of America but our
People are so ashamed.   The signs alter
Our cities serving the sacrament negro
Motion and feelinglanguage logic blood
The jig.   Boss.   Silent, it is without Dracula's
Ease he sucked from the ersatz florentine walls
Something is yet lacking in our people's religion
Said the doctor at midnight

Speaking their own language at that

■

Rejection and the knowledge it is a sense of loss
We lack, that only such emotion could complete us
When we are tired of our thoughtful survival and
Cry to be married to a cringing darkness and capture
It in our own souls.   Petty lunacy of each stilled
Evening in some totally unremarkable place, under-
Stand that as the torture of our rapturous manners

The white glitter of our impressive table
Manners and thoughts that go nowhere after
All we are content to have surround us and

Lift up to the light of our language and
Sip thoughtlessly of the ravishing cup marked
With a brand name of the thing we have used
To identify ourselves on this surprised earth

Minion. The register of surprise at some awkwardly
Pretentious demand
                    breaking up all over again
                        the expectation of some
                      orderly form
The Cross   crucifix
   back
   in the same Dracula
   story

To have been saying, Dracula is a real person
A man
                                        and any Art that depends for sub-
                                                                    stance
                                            there, the human
                                        must end in pieces
                                            appropriate
                                            like the hill

    white stones
and green hill   Athens

The pettiness of a real man
Walks in the luncheonette
Grinning over the sandwich   meat without blood
                                an American
                            Dracula hmmmm

■

A bouquet of ashes.

The Bathers

ONION BUCKET

All silence says music will follow
No one acts under any compulsion
Your story so striking and remain unspoken
Floods in the mind. Each one trying now
To instigate the flutter of light in your
Ear. The voice needling the flashy token
Your presence in some room disguised
As the summer of the leaves. Hilltops
Held by the soft words of the running
Wind. What lie do you need more than this
The normal passion. And each thing says
Destroy one another or die. Like a natural
Introducing here on this plant to Europe
The natural. A piece of furniture, smell
Taste some connection to your earth and
"Realize" nothing more than you need
Another view nothing more than you need yourself
Or that is beautiful. Or your luck that speaks.
Lifting its shoulders out the language
Of the streets. Above. The sky worried
Into its own song. Solid rhythm. She stays
Too close for a letter, scared of a telegram
The finger drum express. Impatient blues.
Anxious blues. Her chemical song loud and
Bright in his dimension. This is the world.
The vegetables are walking.

TWELVE GATES

Face it. The stars have their own lives and care
They are forced into it by your other eye and
Opposite side of your thoughts. Who takes sides
The world quite as fashionable as liars imagined

The picture of one fragile girl in an avalanche
Of the kimono required for their soft trade.
Who is so daring at first to draw lines in the sky
Dingy with this neglected daylight. Opened fan.
Life itself is such a simple thing and we need it

Then here come the music again. And we need that too
People asking each other. The invention of reason.
And those who own nothing what of those walking around
Without land, without cash value, properties. Without

Nothing in their name. Whose destinies
Are not marked or marked down. What of
The ones who are meant to rise in the world
By their names. Whose names are not known.

These worlds are lost in a minute only a gem
Of substance remaining. The necessity to change the form.
These streets clothed in an atmosphere of ash and care-
Less emotion. Who are these persons roll their shoulders

Outside the window in starlight and streetlight
Each young man there reminds the girl of someone
These are the last words I send you for a while.
Written across her fan. Her open eye all flame and
You can feel it take shape in your eye. The lines.

Sufficient confusion calls for a song and
The figure with how many sides. Holler.
Once to the ocean. Sing it for the woman
Whose hands open and deliver the dream

Arousing itself from the day's laborer walking
These streets back from the edge of the river
Deep into town. Traffic. Your voice plays across
The street on the curb right into my open hand

OTHER WORLDS

I see through you in advance!

There are no petty graces
This coffee cup gone cold
Promised recovery. A dutch heart.

What this world is coming to questions and cups.
The song and renewal.

We would rather have you here than absent
Though you fall vomiting into the soup.
We would rather have you here, in English
Than train you in less grand arts of decline

What is not the machine and imposter elevates me
A simple gesture. Not a thought.

This is very important, read it over again

I JUST WANT TO REACH OUT AND BITE YOU BABY

As any time another "hep me"
Addressed to the willing
Stars. And it is effective
Like another fine creature

Beautiful animal just find me
And put her soft life in my hand
For a minute. An hour
Without a second thought

Knowing it is gone be lazy
And gentle and knowing
Everything all about it
You are no big head tonight

Keed. Just sit back there and keep
Your big feet out the dim and
Extravagant journey that puddle
On the floor. Where.

Just because you pretty
When you come in the door
And a temporary genius or star
This one night or nights

Still arriving. Across the way and
Down the alley too. Pretty
Thing. Hungry? And what else
You inquire and think you need

Badly. To "survive" or bullshit
Your way into another eternity
Of less meaningful phrases and
Faces made interesting to junior

Samaritans and other meddlers
Long the road to a wide nose
Jerusalem. In other words, I mean
Why be an idiot of the daytime

Now that everything is so inviting
And so fun. What to do concerts
Nobody in they right mind. Only
When the dark comes on and feeling

Crazy. One tender smile or nod
Bank the belly furnace. Swollen
Tongue. Wanted. Corpulent shadows
Oriental as the goat glaze eye.

Like to walking into the wrong room
Again the tender smile and hands

Under the dumb stars

A smile of beauty cunning
For the exhibition

Such emaciation make all fat people feel good

The compliment of his being
There

THE BATHERS

We turned to fire when the water hit
Us. Something
Berserk regained
An outmoded regard for sanity
While in the fire station
No one thought of flame
Fame or fortune did them

We did them a fortune. We did
Them a favor just being
Ourselves inside of them

Holy day children

In the nation coming your children will learn all about that

But the water creep about us
Water hit us with force.
We saw a boy transformed into a lion
His tail is vau the syllable of love
A master before fellow craft
The summit of the Royal Arch

Lotus. Mover on the face of the waters . . .

        Sleepless Horus, watch me as I lie
Curtained with stars when ye arise
And part the skies. And mount the Royal
Bark

They said the ancient words in shameful English
Their hearts rose up like feathers
In the hidden place

And Horus step into the flood of noon
Shedding his light upon the worlds

It was in Birmingham. It happened.

Week after week in the papers
The proof appeared in their faces

Week after week seeing the same moment grow clearer
Raising the water,

Filling the vessel. Raising the water.
Filling the vessel

O electromagnetic Light shadûf!

Ancient hands bearing water
Ha

The star broke
Over the tub

All righteousness

Not deceived by sunshine nor the light
From a man's desire

Deceived by desire
So that in the moment
The people cast light from their bodies
"Light" being the white premeditation
The simplest fashion
What they want is light

Another source to equip
Their dry want

Want fire light. Space light
Discretions of neon

At least.   So to appear natural
                    Where the sun is

360° of light

Consumed in the labors of comfort
That cries for the balm

Of all that is natural
                            Desire.

Bathing in the dark
The water glowing
In the plastic curtain
Suddenly heated

As another expels past satisfactions.
cold as she washes gas tears
From her man's eyes. We hate you.

Hot on her soft thigh
Like the dog's breath at noon by the Courthouse

We hate you for that

But ancient hands raised
This water

As the street's preachers
Have a good understanding hear them

O israel this O israel that

Down here in this place
Crying for common privilege
In a comfortable land

Their anger is drawing the water
Their daughters is drawing the water.

Their kindness is laving and
Oiling its patients.

That day
                The figures on the trucks inspired no one

Some threw the water
On their heads.
They was Baptists

And that day Horus bathed him in the water
Again

And orisha walked amid the waters with hatchets
Where Allah's useful white men
Came there bearing the water
And made our street Jordan
And we stepped into our new land

Praise God. As it has been since the first time

Through the tear of a mother

THE LION IS THE LAMB

for Ben & Marylin

So that is why you miss certain people
Looking for them

A day. But the impressions
Are so different
Curtis is out on his own
A master, like the man said
On the radio

Ba ba ka ra ba ka
Ab ib rb ra brer
This is what is happening
Life. Ile lfe
The witness:
This is you one two hours ago
Now as real as a snapshot
Coming to Berkeley with the wrong
Magazine
In my hand. No wonder
I am not myself
But I'm learning

Within you
The stars wheel
And cakewalk
As usual, you think up
Something else to complain of
Since the day and the women
Are beautiful

You are not yourself
For which you are thankful

They thinking abt you and things
You know to tell them

They listening to Huey on the radio

Today's lesson in temporary English

We say "you" politely
To avoid pronouncing your name
You are the one and the name
Of you is ancient, magic and powerful
Holy

We want you to be beautiful and
You are.

ANUBIS

A tiger stripped
Of passion
Is not equal
To a dove
The jackal is
A sentry
In his greed
A lamp beneath the mountain
Is a hieroglyph
For love. A man
Should never want
Less than he need

Fit Music

California Songs, 1970

PROEM

When poets beg acceptance for their lines
It's when ephemera and wisdom intertwine
When dull biography engulfs a poem
The poet shores his patron with a Proem
To raise his thought above the dross of life
Since life intrudes, the Proem is a gloss.
Déjà vu more or less. Most likely, more
Should fit you now to hear this song of strife.
You spent childhood rehearsing the Korean War
You fucked up in college and picked the wrong major
And in 66 everyone faked concern for Asia
It was all more fitting than you thought;
The staging. When the orders come down
For the Nam fourth of July as is fitting
You implored the Muses to fly from their knotting
You totaled the Chevy out of meanness
You whined and wondered how to escape this mess
And Lord who to write to. There should be a Lord
If there must be a Proem you thought.
But there was none. Only your drunkard
Friends your dope fiends and pimps
Demon lovers and lovers. And girls dumb
To the morse code from space still arriving
While Zia suns crackled over the desert,
You fled through archives in your brain
Remembering acidulous hash and devotions
Consecrated by the pain of navigating through wine
In peaceful East Coasts full of bare bodies
And icy streets under neon. Now tropical death
Leaped before you. You wept. Wastefulness when
The car ran them down. And the orders came down
As your prophets demanded. Strange FM stations
And astrological phonecalls hastened to soothe you,
Saying, "don't give a damn." It was time
To be going. Vancouver or South Viet Nam.

And Kung said, "Without character you will
be unable to play on that instrument
Or to execute the music fit for the Odes."
—*Ezra Pound,* Canto XIII

FIT MUSIC

I

Moon rays like pure snow

What here on this coast three ahem and wine bottles
Shining in the trash
This is my concern for the day
And something new in the evening
Another beautiful whore
Make me grateful O Lord

There is a time for everything
Let alone getting high

What. Here in beautiful California
The surf remembers another form
Of revolution. Nothing. But what
Else do you want to remember

Catherine or the note tacked up on the wall
Where is Bethesda I am lost

. . . .

II

Wait. What is astrology when people still fucking up
Daily

. . . .

III

And still it is helpful to be here
Gifted. Solemn. Ridiculously macho
This effeminate county. What
Remains is to be bargained away
For another souvenir medallion

The truth

So thank you Cathy we will get together and smoke dope
Another evening. Maybe tomorrow

And thanking lucky stars too

Sending back reports from the seaside

Sun Yat Sen's final telegram

Sorry, all that
is CLASSIFIED

We not too sure where you'll be
When worlds collide

Sending back reports from the seaside

. . . .

IV

Ooooh oooh. Nothing the magic in the air
We call this aether. Magic and
Science. Shut em down shut em down

But all you want is another
Beautiful whore. A good thing

I am glad you are with me here
And wherever I roam. My friends
Thank you. And love for you

In this place. I am glad the radioactivity
Registers

In my flesh there is the sound
Beaming forth from the glass
As she traces the ring of the bottle
With her soft hands. Smiling
And scheming

There is something (History) about you
White women and
Spanish girls
Passing for white

. . . .

V

I rejoice for this island

I rejoice for this island, I climb
South Hill to pick the turtle-fern,
All alone here
Who shall not pine

I see my official friends
They are also complaining

Yet Confucius went on plucking the *k'in* and
Singing the Odes.

Ezra Pound, certified madman
Is melancholy. In his book
On the shelf. Overdue. What
A mean life

VI

This is stupid. This is very stupid.
No one but Anne will understand
When I hand her these songs, when

I put my hand to my lips and concentrate on your mistakes
How you bumped into the wrong individuals
In the saloon. And kept on smiling right on

Sending back reports from the beach

Sending back reports from the seaside

. . . .

VII

Among the reasons why the beach is beautiful is
The music on the radio is alright
Because it has nothing to do with you
And still it reminds me of something

Has to do with you,

Cathy

On my way to Vietnam. And loving
Your dope too

La Jolla

Where even the freaks ask dumb questions about you

San Clemente

When Worlds Collide on TV

That is our talk here; sweating
And dirty

Where through the wood a moiré ribbon
Runs

Speeding linnet and the circling crow
Above

Pendleton
Studying war

. . . .

VIII

First gear it's alright
Second gear. Lean right
Third gear, hang on tight
Faster

It runs the hills like a mattress
Cause my Honda's built
Really light. When I go in
To the turns

Better hang on tight

I better turn on the light so we can ride
My Honda tonight

That is what's happening in the time warp

. . . .

IX

    Live up to your clothes,
Sd K'ung Fu Tse

Despite what we learned
Of the sins of the suburbs
And the dreams of the harbor

Standing for their irrational anthems

        December enters the world
Collusion

Sagittarius

                        An ignorance and circumstance

              Somehow involve me
                  in their Fathers' greed

The soft spots in the city
Or 5th Street's sulking faggot bars

        Above the spirits smoke and noise
When worlds collide

X

The old man has to look up
From the chess board. Such
Music come out the Odes
And it's so beautiful now

And Maria in the morning crosses my mind the beach is so beautiful
Because of the Chinese spy in the greenhouse

The sun people bleach their hair in the sun

If I mention Isis they ready to fight

XI

I thought how my friend Ted went from Toshiro Mifune
To deep respect for those people

But they are not the same people!

Is there no other way
From the madness
Of National City?

Trying to wake up in the old woman's bed
For another taste of salt air

Out there in this odd California
There is no science fiction

XII

Your San Diego
Mission Beach
Made me stand up
To a gun 9mm Luger

For the whore in this white cathy

The words the facts so easily gathered
Tonight. It is the creature we both love
I want to hear from you tomorrow
Let alone getting high. And really

This beach is beautiful

San Diego 1970

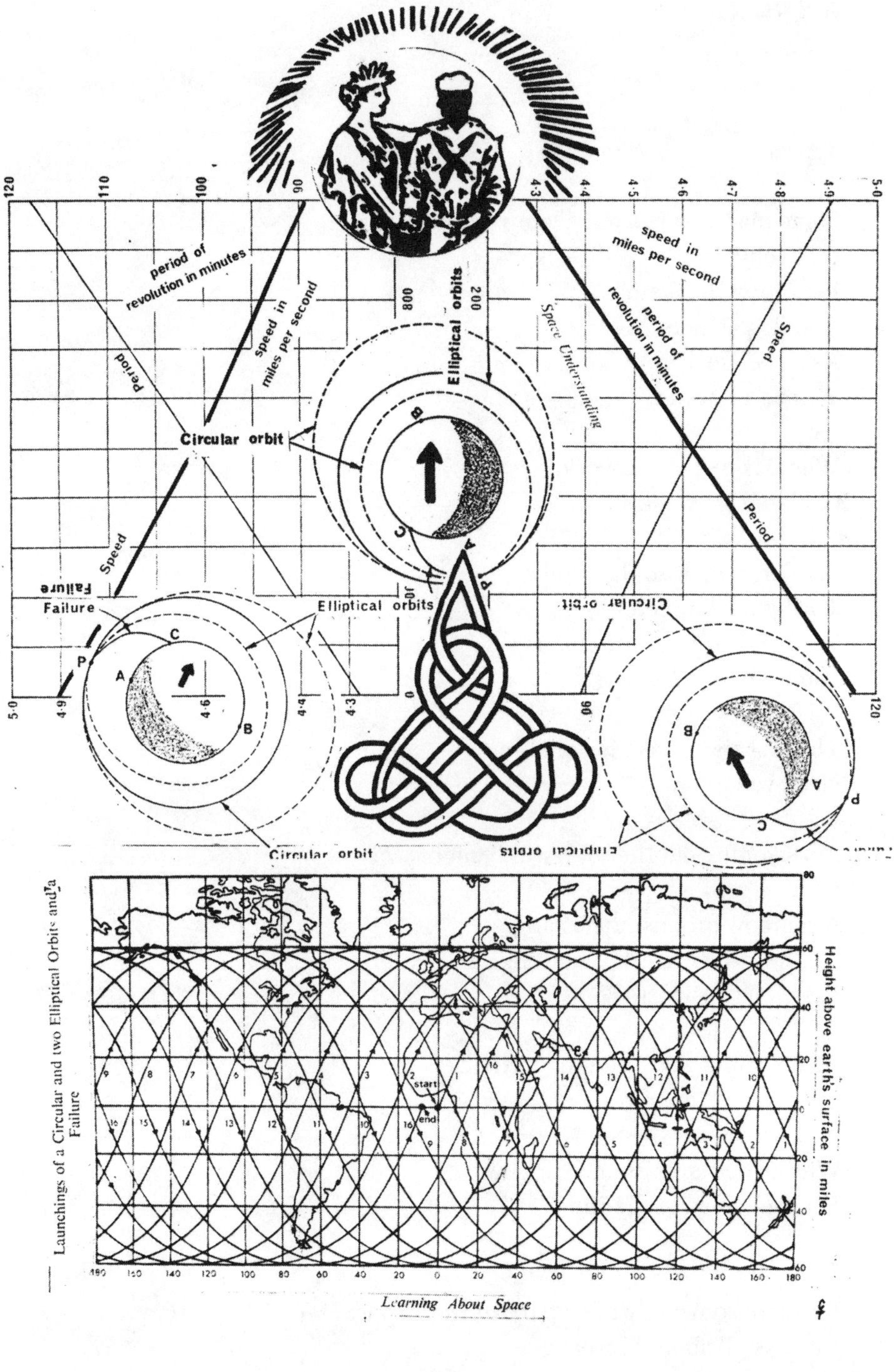
period of revolution in minutes
speed in miles per second
Period
Speed
Circular orbit
Elliptical orbits
Failure
speed in miles per second
period of revolution in minutes
Speed
Period
Space Understanding
Launchings of a Circular and two Elliptical Orbits and a Failure
Height above earth's surface in miles
start
end
Learning About Space

ENVOY

Typical.

Some madman has put a lamp on the ceiling
Of Boeing 707s
Depicting the Wain
And its partners
As if they seen
Through a turret

Where is this in the world?
Can't tell from the stars

Suddenly, I felt so thankful
The lights dimmed
We dropped from the clouds
San Francisco looked up

The first sight was McDonald's
Neon yellow arc

A beckoning out the cold, windy night

A rainbow promising nothing
And warning that that nothing
Is serious business

That nothing was bringing me back
Back to de Plantation!

Why all de slaves am not singing
For the return of the Kid

■

I wanted somebody to stop me at the airport
And ask all about Vietnam

But nobody asked me
What did you find out
About Jesus,
Was it worthwhile did you have fun
As it says in the song making me
Suffer was it fun
Making me suffer
Now I want to know

Did you by lucky chance
Buy a camera a stereo deck

How did you like being the envoy of a monstrous epic
Or saga of Western corruption
When the white guys blacked their mugs
Before the ambush, what did you do kid?

Who was that dancehall girl

How come you think
You made a difference to her
To me to them to what huh
What are you A egotist huh
B patriot C idiot D huh

When you thought that your presence
Might somehow stay a more cruel hand
The mentality behind that
Is something in this world

There is one photograph of the Kid in his camouflaged
Cowboy hat

The sponsors of that program
Must not have another word,

Not even when I get finished ranting

Slum Days after the War

WONDERS

I know where I belong
But I been away so long.
Sometimes I wonder.
Will I ever hear
Nostalgia in Times Square
Again, in some Avenue B
Break-in 2 bath flat
Will I ever sit
In the sun, high
On a Lennox terrace
And watch the Harlem River run
Away from the dope
And the crime
To the gray East
Again? And me
With some Boone's Farm
Meaning no harm
On anybody
Sitting there digging
Eddie Palmieri's
Hip conversations
With Obatala.
Sometimes I wonder
About that.
Or to be freak again
Be in the Bronx
Stoned on the rocks
As Jr Walker strain
His voice and young girls' credulity. Again?
Oh girls I can hear
Your radios
Loud at midnight
In Harlem or Elmhurst
And the smog a gangster
To ask proud

Stars give it up.
Girls
Check it out
When you pout and talk bad
Think of me, exiled
Almost a year
From the life
Lord, and don't be so hard
Sometimes I be distracted
When I think how you style.
Hold it. I sound like
The Browning of America!
I feel so simple to be thinking of Harlem
New York, the apple
Where we had our own Adam
And damn near all
The wonders of the world

Saigon, VNCH

ENLIGHTENMENT

You cannot sleep.
They say, at last
You wake up
Now you think like them

You have caught the lotus, overcoming
And the dove

Spiritual studies bore you
Over listless afternoons

Awareness of Tuesdays and
Thursdays

Limbs greasy with insomnia, you arrive
In the one cloud
Above the river
Which is the whole sky

O slender Lord Buddha

Now deference
And cupped hand
Or mudra. For everybody
Spirit body
Nor how unworthy they be

They were more devoted to their lives
Sad or sordid, still an exercise
In something. Being. Spirit. Duty

Drunkenness
And drug-borne ahimsa. They say:

It’s so nice
You have some loutishness in you
Your former mildness
Was a source of pain

We are foolish enough to still give you a card
On your birthday

Please say thank you

I go all over town, shoving people
In buses

But I am not holy.
I want my money back
When I don’t ride.

SURVIVORS

You didn't used to comfort
None but the mourning

Things is changing. Now
Everyone need
Consolation and

Veterans of fiendish wars
Wear the poppy in they arms

They seize their pension from your cars
Their disability repay
A gluttonous trust. The one
Blue window in your room
Replays your inhumanities
With mad canister laughter

Despite ampule warnings
College kids blowing themselves up
With crystal reefer
O my Lord, O my Lord

People. Let's make a deal

America would be beautiful
If you willing to trade
And go speaking proverbs
Like peasants everywhere

Junkies is beautiful respected in all other lands
As men of peace someone like God
Must have a crush on. Or something.

HEAVENLY BODIES

My stares cause
No disturbance
To my stars. They
Accustomed to rude forms of flattery
They don't mind me

I'm using the 4 principle
Till things get better
When I seek them, I think
How remarkably lovely

How can I trust omens that dance with such grace
In this ugly place
God sure loved the negro
To give him America

As here and there
In grave cities
Gélés interrupt
The commuters. Bellatrice
Eloquent in a gesture, gélés
Sprouting. The tricks
Of Osiris awakening up

It is still cold in the sun
And this is Easter

In New York the typists are so beautiful
They deserve love stories of their own

Solitude is a falsehood
It's my stars too polite

A telepath roams through Duffy Square
Confusing the sex shows
And no one knows why this is

You wouldn't think of walking out
On the street

FAITH

She said she don't want no man
In her house. But
She ain't yet called
On God to notarize

Anything. And she smiled
So beautiful

She was 122 per cent black
Except for calling on God

Someday it may happen you will lose
Something so precious
To you you will say Jesus

But you will not ask me to go

THE HEROIN OF MY YOUTH

I refuse to pass my swellings off for
authentic glories.
—Aimé Césaire

Time goes on. And it's a gas!
I'm so glad. In three weeks
I will be finished being a youth
Though I will not give up you,

Will not give up playing ball in the park
Or being a all night dancer
I will gain the first pension
Of memory. Let me tell you

In my youth, I stood on the corner
Discussing zip gun specifications

In your youth Revolution was a topic
Even though we knew they had tanks
And thousands of unemployed whiteboys
Impatient to storm through the park.

What was that?
Sometimes I myself find it
So hard to figure out
What I'm actually doing

Once I played gigolo to the white witch
What was that? What was that about?

I know I know better than that
Still I really got into that
When she touched me I used to say
Ohwoo oughoo uh doo doo uhh uhh.

GRANDPA'S SPELLS

There is a place beyond the reach
Of search or accident

Days the people sleeping late
The sun unrolls the awnings

There is a five-barred gate. A graceful
Hill almost perplexes the street
A memory strolls in the mornings

It's not exactly the best
Example of city planning
As become fashionable these days.

The situation is as bad in the East
Where the people love poetry
And where one secret book says:

The jewel of life floats in its superior element.
The truth of the eye
It is a notorious thing

People thought up music and magic
To say:

You a child of the Mother

They thought up diamonds. And gold.
Invented hieroglyphs and
Traveled space with the Blues

You goes there when you just don't know what else to do

Your heart yearning,
It hurt you to beg her

But now you don't know what else to do
What can you do what
Conjure star-rise
Sooner than the code

Of a tear. Maybe something is wrong
With tradition
Teaching us that

O starlight, what must I do that would shift you

What suns must I begin tuning
To dry up these tears

HISTORIOGRAPHY

Bird is a god of good graciousness.
—Ted Joans

I

The junkies loved Charlie Parker and the sports
And the high living down looking ones
Those who loved music and terror and lames
Who in Bird's end would someday do better

As the Bird spiraled down in disaster
Before the TV set some would come to prefer
Out of the sadness of Mr Parker's absence
Never again hearing the strings of Longines

Symphonette

Without hearing the keening cry of the Bird
Nailed to the wax they adored. In the memories
And warmth of their bodies where our Bird
Stays chilly and gone. Every cat caught with

A white girl wailed Bird Lives! And the dopies
Who loved Charlie Parker made his memory live
Those who loved music made his memory live
And made the young ones never forget Bird

Was a junkie

. . . .

II

We lost others to pain stardom and
Some starved at vicious banquets
Where they played until the victuals
Was gone. Pretty music. For all that

Pain. Who made the young ones remember the pain
And almost forget the dances? Who did that?
Steal the prints and the master and burn down
The hope of his rage when he raged? It was

Not only pain

There was beauty and longing. And Love run
Down like the cooling waters from heaven
And sweat off the shining black brow. Bird
Was thinking and singing. His only thought

Was a song. He saw the truth. And shout the Truth
Where Indiana was more than the dim streets of Gary
A hothouse of allegedly fruitful plain America
Some will never forgive the brother for that. Bird

Was a junkie

. . . .

III

According to my records, there was something
More. There was space. Seeking. And mind
Bringing African control on the corny times
Of the tunes he would play. There was Space

And the Sun and the Stars he saw in his head
In the sky on the street and the ceilings
Of nightclubs and Lounges as we sought to
Actually lounge trapped in the dull asylum

Of our own enslavements. But Bird *was* a junkie!

LINER NOTES

Because it is conceived as a tonal evocation of the spirit of Charles Parker (1921–1955), “Historiography” is a poem designed for oral recitation. It is a solo constructed in the bop saxophone style. The poem was written to be performed with a jazz orchestra of 3–7 pieces, using traditional 1940s bebop instrumentation. In its own way, the poem is an investigation of the sonic developments pioneered by Parker and his associates.

“Historiography” has been performed in New York City sittin’ in with the Wes Belcamp group at the Village Door (1972) and with the Ric Murray Trio on a poetry and jazz program entitled *UNION* at Sir James’s Pub (April 18, 1974). The piece has also been performed with Lanny Steele and the Texas Southern University Jazz Ensemble at the Westheimer Art Fair in Houston, Texas (September 1974).

BROTHER ME

You don't call them heroes

A hero a dead man
In Greek. And
Cincinnati Ohio

Call them son of a gun
Brother me

When you sing sing the vowels

The biography is just
Like any mythology:

The star was seen in daylight in Peking
A light 6,000 years
To reach the earth. Star
It was seen in Phu Nhuân

In daylight along Hai Ba Trung

And you was not supposed to have been there

Saturday morning before lunch
Among other invisibles

Including the miracles
Coerced from the sky

With photographs taken several hundred
Years apart. Seeing invisible stars

Who saw us laughing
In the mud. High.
And playing handball
In schoolyards vanishing
Toward the nebulas

What they doing
They had to be
Looking at brother
Me from up there,
Sure they did

Admiring us, since we bursted from the same flesh
Before they sent us here on this mission

Beautiful
Lamp-post graduates
In weird gaming rags
We changed

Like persons in ancient Abyssinian stories
Mistranslated in the schools we avoided

Dropped out. Nodded out
Joined the Army and styled
In OD. Starlike and black
To the max to the onion

Baby Pimp and Dopie Jr, Rag Eddie and Judo
And Stuff stuff

And only the stars them did see us
Once the bô-áts accepted
Our histories in a handshake

Dap making *my den* invisible, brother me

Sad and fortunate tales
In a gesture,

Proclaiming it's no longer charming
To murder a brother
Well trained to murder

We was well trained in the heavens,
Well trained in the World
But still we children of the Mother

As once we illumined the summer
A very long springtime is coming
Choreographed in the stars long ago
It is coming

We still be children of the Mother
We are the serpent guerillas   waiting
When the darkly flourishing son
Bring his canteen back to the River
We will be ready

Then, as we were then

As we jitterbugged
To the ballcourt
As we escaped from the stupid harangue
Of our white televisions
In quiet or righteous or desolate
Or deafening homes. Fled
Into a dream of crime and
Manhood, as any other boys

But we was coming from neighborhoods
Like Ná'ir al Dabarán

Never had time to be boys

And some days will come better light radiate from this star
And no songs for Lord Death
Or landscape of possible dying

A long springtime is coming
So long ago star blessed
Starring brother me, singing
For the Creator. At last.

Singing for the Creator at last

SEA OF CHANCE (A SAILOR SONG)

"She have a sailor man ..."
—S. Francisco

The light made her beautiful
To behold. It was illusion.
But that is a function of light
As some who are lucky can see.

NIGHT AND DAY

All illusion competes.

Underwater and away out in space
This light is more beautiful

HER MIRROR IN HER HAND

She's beautiful in the light of his eyes
And all that mattered was trashed
In her train when she forgot to raise
The hem of her garment. Stylish one!

She was more beautiful to him than light

MORE BEAUTIFUL THAN STARS

She had the eyes of the Mother
And a heart flowing stone.
This woman was out of sight

IN THE NAVY WE CALL THAT A SEA STORY

You hear. You wonder how he got there?

BOÖTES

Arcturus shined. As Hesiod sang
That was the time to pluck
The cluster from the vine
He packed up and left home.

He cast his fortunes on the lap
Of the sweet sea

Thank you so much, Mr Hesiod

WINKING, SHE HALF-OPENS HER BOOK

That is a remarkable picture
Of the process. I know it.

You come into your memories this way
Like a ship out of Roosevelt Roads

Such is life's character and form. Unfolding.

THE UNFOLDING

Childishly, memory leaps up
From the lap of the sitter
Wanting to play out in the rain

Childishness

An adult comes in out the rain and sensibly opens
His umbrella to dry it. Then
The phone rings or Arcturus
Rises. Time to be going again

The rain has stopped

His galoshes impatiently tap
The umbrella openly preens

STRUTS

A black pavanne recalling African Spain
In its corner reminding him to take it

Just in case. He folds it up
Where all that magic went?
I mean naturally African Spain
Shall that be unfolded again

Are such wonders anywhere to be found?

ALL DAY ALL NIGHT MARYANN (A SAILOR SONG)

Out of Norfolk to Puerto Rico you are halfway to Spain
And pain; magnet memories that sting like brine

LIBERTY

Gypsies!

ZERO FOR CONDUCT AS USUAL

They checked all of the stalls:
No guidebooks to the B-girls

April in the Free World

Dididahdit dahdahdah dahdahdah didahdidit   Fool!

THE FAMOUS DOOR

For worthy painters loitering in Spain
Afternoons of red wine in a café in Rota

This door became a still life and a circus.
Waxed fruit. Sangria. Exciting near-death
As two white hands strain toward the swinging bar

Delicate, finished, feminine hands
Turned the knob to Love's fast hour

HE SAW AUNT MARY COMING AND HE JUMPED BACK IN THE ALLEY

Radio songs flushed a narrow la calle

And the fleet in the harbor wanes to sea
Vanishing like the G on the tourist's
Finger on the hand the urchin had held

Out on deck the Free World sailors cry to Venus
Below, some skaters practice cheating cards.

ANCHORS AWEIGH

We foamed around her throne

"WHY THEY CALL A SHIP A SHE"

Huh a slip of the lip

Once pledged to follow where our Lady leads
He couldn't get that idee out of his head

She pulled him back and forth
Through his devotion's froth

But then his memory wakened a hometown
Complete with songs by Charles Brown

Brooklyn Navy Yard. He jumped ship.

He sang, "Well huh I'm drifting and drifting"
Driven by Fortune he found himself ashore
Where he stood lost, amused by what he saw.

THE TAROT OF THE BOHEMIANS

People shuffled around in bellbottoms and beads
Hoping for new exotic ways of living
In New York's lonely glass shell. Dead

Sounds drove any sweet soft voice to hell
And all the people back to the wall
Wanting to be both SLY 121 and forgiving

JUST YOU JUST ME

They swore not to dislike the other tenants.
They swayed through dirty streets like
Drugged anemones. In uniform remnants,

He rocked and rolled all along Avenue B
Now uh somewhat different from memory
But not that much. Peered in the Shipwreck
Saloon through its fashionable "porthole"

MURMURED IN TOMPKINS SQUARE PARK

No one interesting there. But in Tompkins Sq Park
A grounded siren whispered to his soul
Beneath the besmogged stars. He heard
The ocean speak. No, it was only a bird.

He sure was hard-headed

SUGAR HILL

How you like that?

Quadrasonic baby

When you turn these speakers up
Behind this music
A breeze actually blows
Through the room. Man!

That's how come I believe engineers
Truly exist

Though we cannot see them

FLY SOCIETY

Telling no stories that is no lies
She will talk till last call.
She mentions nineteen highpriced
Islands

Visited all in one summer. All lies.
Entertaining if you understand the need
Sneakily she be trying to tell you

You are a fool to be here
In one place and a young
Pretty dude. She would take you to Bermuda
And pay the Hotel

You so stupid you would buy her a drink
Experience tells her no no thank you

You lose

In the next booth drinking exhibits its curse
The smiles are left in the Bar
To tangle so sad with the legs
The upturned chairs on the tables

All the drinkers so sad. S Halsted St parade

They return home to resume arguments
The minor conflicts of connubial life

Alcohol of some sort
Preens in their blood

And those ignorant statements at home
Fueled by the persistent Blue Flame

TO SPEAK OF WOE THAT IS IN MARRAKESH

Tramp! Well, you can call me that
—Lowell Fulson

She turned on CSN&Y
She unrolled another roll
Of Reynolds Wrap across

The windows
Then she told me

A funny story of a girl

Singer she had "personally known"
Strange scenes in Daly City.

A gold mine of information!

Around the corner at TV NEWS
Are magazines from everywhere
She's ever been. A few from
Other different places too.

She speaks of a VW van in Amsterdam

She smiles & winks & sings to me
"Hey don't you know you're riding"

Hell. Don't you *see* me riding?

BETTER PHYSICS

I

Anyone who love you
Can keep you

And they will know how to move you

They will touch you
With their hands
Lightly. They will
Give messages
To the sun when
You are distant

Or the stars, when the time
Change

Someone who loves you will know
How to move you
With annoyance and
Incredible graces
They can move you,
They once built pyramids
With they power.

There are other things
You must know:

Creatures that hate you
Will try to remove you

While madness reigns, they will try to remove you
They will try to displace you

Knowing once the Creator
Have set you in motion
There is no way to replace
You

    You have your place
In all my days and dreams

When you love someone you promise
Them moments and days
When you love them enough

Love returns love. Love makes agreements and compromise
And rearrange space
Like you do with time
Someone who love you
And anyone who you love

When you love someone your hand
In the air is a love letter,

As plain as an E
A moment you gave

That's what I thought when I lifted my hand

II

There are moments I love
More than midnight. Already,
The sunlight that was in me
Awakens

Every thought of you naturally grows
From where you sat on the chair
When the boat eased back toward
Kampuchea. And you were not there

There is a god, when pain is a blessing

There are women you've made
Beautiful

Moving you about

In the game of their bodies

There is something I don't like about theories of moving things

So prevalent in the world
When I'm in it

Sometimes, I feel
Like breaking
Somebody's back

There is something I also dislike about figures
Of speech that tempt you to misunderstand.

What we need in this world is a better physics

How could I mean to hurt her

WHILE MADNESS REIGNS

These madmen have ruined the Age
Not even they are content

Things perish, begging
The sky for rebirth

Mountains demand RSVP and
Poisons flood the clouds
The Fishes ignore everyone
In their portable ocean

That is beauty given for pain. Bread
Wars astonish the people

Kill them too.
They want someone to talk to
Even if just to complain
That their history lies all
Degenerate under the cough
And the nasality of the flowers

Wanting someone to talk to

A young girl turns
To a tree in the sunlight
This is magic, a world
And relation. The tree
Chokes and dies in the air
This is madness and greed

Science fails. Other witchcrafts become monsters
While people starving for love
For affection. For lunch. Crying:
Skill is no longer sufficient
Nor efficiency, nor politeness

The curse has fallen now on the mad;
Their children purposely starving
To widen the scope of their minds
Asking them poisoned Asian riddles

Must they seek madness
Now to tool eternity
Conspicuously invisible
Among the lustful dead
Organization? Mass whoredom.

From my closet in the anonymous kingdom
I wondered can this be
The very mysterious planet
Of sunlight shadow and rain

The shimmering light of the Fishes' annoyance

Even after they destroy it
There are subtle affects
Of the air and the weather
Light sunlight shadow rain

Not even these madmen can duplicate it
Learn Zen to remain unforgiven
Destroying life to make a living
So proudly, while madness reigns.

SERPENT GUERILLAS

The vipers advance

Another sector illumined
The 5th of the 14th Quadroons moving up
The azmadj slid forward
In a powder white El Dee

Under the blue eyes of the police
And the daily defenders of the cuff-
Link and 504 necktie regime
They did not see the advance

They wondered at the rolling eyes
Of the 3rd Minstrelsy
But allowed them to pass
They did not understand

What was incorrectly defined as a truce
After the scenario of Merit
And Love brought us casualties
We could not afford. Our King

Fell there

Remember the day, brothers and
All the other unseasonal nights
Nights of flame, days of fire
At the water cooler, forget.
Springs of pain summers of glittering
Eyes. Say nothing more when they ask

Now what can they want
Again, demonstrations

As they will have nerve to ask
Then smile all the way back home
To the suburbs as you get on the bus
And return to Headquarters
Children playing in sunlight
More squalid than it had been

Young troops in the doorways, nodding
as you pass in review
The 189th Wine Bottleers
Saluting as you go past

Someone from Maintenance or Procurement eases
Into the Bar with another blond captive.

As you tear off your tie and the soot in the air
Nationalizes your collar, you
Will wonder what in the hell
Madmen like me have been saying

But this is only our first Spring offensive
Though it may seem

The Inner City, used to recoil
Now stretches out
Another new Science
With more spiritual tests
In the superior centers
Of commerce, the seasons
Are accounted for, one madness must admit
Another or lose
A sheriff on you
Spying for one gasp of wit
The Inner City conquers
And, to reprovoke a new rule
Orchestrate it
Call it a blues   yessir

When you ready
Battle Plan: mercy
Goes into effect
We are not fixing to die
We shall conquer without a doubt!
We shall conquer
Without a doubt
All this death hides
Something so vital
Everyone cannot be permitted
To see what has happened.

WORK SONG

And what I now say with one tongue, tomorrow will say with many
—Kahlil Gibran

Asson
Sing with me now

Asson e yiho! You
Sing with me now

All of you who are now under
the sound of my sight
You who listen see a new view
You who can sign hear
Voices as many as stars
Who talk that talk
Catches numerous as twigs
On a tree. Breath light
As clouds and tunes as beautiful
As ripples in a lake or pool

River in a glass in you an eye
Ring
Changing that way this way
Same same and unpredictably the same
Old song for a new who of you
Uh we a who a me a you a us a who

Sing this work song sung with a high voice
Bass voice all harmonies between
For the Creator. Out of the troubles
Of this world
Hush. Listen. Troubled voices say:

We work all day. With or without pay.
They spread the pyramids we build
To crucify us. We soldier well and they

Return us frozen hearts and fallen stars
And etch taps into our circle of sound

Their rhythms have worried our bones
Into flutes of obscene death-pale tones
Deafening the people of Earth
To the harmonies of their worth

Who   people of Earth.

Being. More dear than sunlight
Pricelessness could be their debut
If their bodies could let them see
And their eyes let them hear who we are
Through deep channels ringing our star

We put our ear to the sky
And listen only for silence
Subtle pulse of our hearts
An attraction. To guide us

When we have grown tired of silence
And the misery of our own function
The stars bring their music to soothe us
As always. When we are the miserable ones.

Who

We are the miserable people
Knowing whatever we do
Only hurts so. So what
Can we do
Afternoon we are dreaming
A neon communist dream
In the street May Day in September
Labor Day we all say
To show we are loyal
At least to the larger

Schemes of the law we accept
And its criminal orders
As we actually use our own money
Chicken change
To ride bridges and trains
They tax us and toll
Us for the fruit of our toil
Like shamed virgins in coffles
We perspire in subways
Waiting for our one day

Dreaming. The workers hug the new victors
And the blue floats which laughingly carry
The old governors to their arrest
Down dizzy avenues to the recovered
Reviewing stand where the people stand
Infinite legions of us. Those who toil

Perhaps we need to brush up on "extortion"

Huh. That dream so cold in the light

Asson. Sing with me now
Beyond my patois confusion
So wretched we stand now
From an ancient displacement
Will not never ever forget the criminal insults
Who?

The further arrogance of these men
Who claim to rule by our consent
By wiretap by felony ruse and lie
Strongarm and terror in plain suits
Uniform standardization of death
Briefcase bug drug and waged spy
The ecstasies of their usual business
And supersonic rape of any beauty.

Which means Victor Hugo was happier in Paris
Than I am now in New York never hearing the stars
Sing their workshops or chansons of space joy
Because the news keeps blunting the starwaves

Telling how much our rulers really hate us
Who toil. How they use us and care less how
Much they hurt us. So that if we will have
Ecstasy of our own it is dreaming only revenge

We who cannot love without stars
Who love sunlight. We needs a tool

To pull out the taps in space where they plugged
Our sphere into turmoil.

O how the "masters of the world"
Have failed us the ones who toil

We shall surely unpower these criminal lords.
May the Creator be pleased with our songs

FRAMING THE SUNRISE

Satellite countries

appearing with anachronistic pomp or tragedy
in living rooms

where a magazine is thrown carelessly
                                        by the sofa
Family Circle

where a lazily circling black disc
spins Charles Earland into the space
of the room's life
                joyful intensity
overdriving
                solemn middle American words
about mortars and dyings

The state of the art is improving

One subtle breeze drums sweetly through the screen

blinking at the edge of each image
                                    phantom
A war that is finished
as far as America is concerned
hangs in the air like a ghost

Justify
        BRIGHTNESS   COLOR

The state of the art
                    is improving

indian paintbrush follows the road
                                washes hillsides

bluebonnets
numerous as electrons

The state of the art
simple spring blooms
scanning memory
improving the grounds of our vision
reflection on the state

remember the mirror-image days
the FDR set at Hyde Park
outside Poughkeepsie's perpetual chill

a Philco?

remember the technical shakedown
Elizabeth Two's coronation
the excellent march on Lam Son

surplus camouflaged maimed
ARVN vets

the colorful Beefeaters
Grant Park mounted police

Caroline's jumper remember Selma
the bridge

colorful b&w 8mm teargas clouds
from Budapest
by satellite relay

bullets from Kent State Ohio
by outrage

from Belfast, bombings on videotape

Queen Soraya
by an inch

The state
of the art
is improving
remember the thrilling firefights
during supper
you could afford Safeway meat
Morley Safer
trying to tell Mama
you getting ahead on the job
remember "Tell Mama"
Eddie Fisher's Coca-cola dance party
Jocko on channel 13
when it was really educational
the Shirelles came in
via Public Service bus
& lip-synched the first 45

doo run doo run do run

rice
paddies with antiphonetical names

Ike mispronouncing "veet numb"
Korean frostbite Yalu River

Thursday night with John K. M. McCaffery
brought to you
by Chase National Bank

Thursday night channel 5
11 o'clock news
roll calls
local high school kids
dead

dead 9 years before their reunions

dead Lance Cpl regalia
dying on *CBS NEWS*

via satellite relay
dying
anchorman death

yearbook/basic training photograph front page Friday
Long Island Press
by the school or survivors

one-legged Joe Pyne
cussing the soft-spoken ones
hair

The fan in the window shudders slightly
summer night
gnats escadrille on the porch
around the bug light

dead bootcamp photograph
retouched on the console
cheap imitation gold frame turning russet
as this August lengthens nightly

dead Ft. Jackson smile
pyramid-based
on a sorrowful doily
deserted

Yes he should have.

remember the festive gold knobs
on the Magnavox of live assassinations

rhododendrons saying shadow
for any trace of sunlight on their leaves
by the window

"The Man" on the moon
remember plastic American flags

doo run doo run do run

dream coolness of Dalat
holy crumbling walled Hue
Vung Tau bikini
Bikini

former President Truman
in ½ life
strolling
New York spring dawns
early b&w sun
reflecting
into rimless glasses
look just like
little Orphan Annie
in Missouri drag

ain't he

remember slowmotion humanoid dummies
disintegrating
at ground zero
at White Sands
at newsreel Nagasaki
Copenhagen or *Skoal!*

White Heat with Jimmy Cagney
Late late night

"Tell Mama"

We lived with this shit twenty years
and each became monsters
lazy unfeeling
brutally corrupted by our senses
crazy pride regained
crazy before & after

slate dark winter sky
                                    and one fuzzy star
like an Admiral's magic eye
                                                fading after the Nitecap
reiterated disasters sleep
                                            & "God Give Us This Day"

and wonder what shall we accomplish
                                                        or resign
framing the sunrise
                                    this time during the Late News

The state of the art is improving
our most homely inattention
to the horror existing
                                    in our nameless wonder
            via satellite
                        entire countries

I tell you and tell you

I tell you   we was framed!

FĀTIHA

Al sibu tutashinda mo bila shaka!

As the cellblock has its muezzin
You hear the call
To liberate the mind
Riffs of vision,

Haste of worry thought and
Desperation of radio
Ballads so very slowly
Escaping the circled

Days. Exceedingly slow
1¾ ips six or seven ideas in an hour
Blessing of non-activity
Blessing of pertinent time

And to me power
Heh heh heh

Rock floats in the caged air
But the riff is power
In one of myriad worlds
Science of privacies,

Domains. Consider this technology
Of liberation. Consider this
Emission of the mantic force
And grace. Our serpents our sun

As even the Pope has a scarab
As even someone unworthy as me has the key
This star is our planet
And yes, we shall be free

Euphemysticism

A SONG FOR THE BANANA TREE SLEEPING IN MY YARD

It's a good thing
trees can't sing

They'd be like us!

So it's a good thing
that trees cannot sing

They only stand & see
what humans do

If they could
sing they'd say
O SINNER MAN
WHERE YOU GONNA RUN TO

Where "Moonlight Madness"
at Dept stores provides
sane and maintainable debaucheries
for the employed and wise

O SINNER MAN WHERE YOU GONNA HIDE

Where others buoy perdition
on the installment plan
of Tavern tabs and
daily all-night fun

uh-huh

They only stand or bend
they cannot run

And it's a damned good thing
trees can't sing

COSMIC COMMUNION

I received a thought from you
Sent dancing
Subtly as incense

The magnetic magician spoke
Of the wheel of Life:

"Just like a song

You are capable
Of deep incredible
Vastly beautied
Conceptions

You will grow bodies
Strong and filled
With love and gleam
Like stars"

Selah

"Those I'm now touching,

Name your new dances
After flowers and trees

Compose popular songs
For air currents,

Be on a first name basis with planets
And stars

They will know you
Are beautiful like them

You will hear yourselves
Speaking and it will be
Like a song. You will be

You must remember this
As you awaken."

BLUES CADET

after Sonnyboy Williamson

I'd rather take flying lessons.

I've worn out the pictures on the carpet
Just pacing my room

Ever since you went away
My life's portion of gloom
Increased a thousand fold

And in my four-walled room around me
The walls are closing like a door.

PAUL LAURENCE DUNBAR VIEWS THE SWORD OF TOUSSAINT L'OUVERTURE, CHICAGO EXPOSITION 1893

for Etheridge Knight

Four hundred years of exploitation
Edged the blade

And black Toussaint exposed
The rent in white imperial veils
As the tropic sky burst with
Dark thunder and the lightning

Of the saints. Orisha from Guinee.

Ogoun unchained
The blade before his eyes
Cut down and cleared

Perfumed materialism of Versailles
And flicked the latch for Legba

Where spirits wandered on the razor edge
A king's highway

Open the jails! Undo the chains!

Spirits loosed in the world and slaves
Set free. And young Paul's tongue
A floating in his mouth struck blind

The hatred with our common speech,
Yes it will come St. Paul will come will come
To us as once to you so young and gaping

Before the opening of a better world.

EUPHEMYSTICISM

His eyes scratched reflection
On the window's glass
And filled it with wine
Candlelight and gitano
song poems

White wine Tyrolia
That dream disarmament

Over and over again
Always again his procession
Unreeling

As she steps down from the train

In the background
As exhaust fills the station
Under the beautiful glass

Ribbed and vaulted;
In the middle ground passengers
Walking and going walking
From coming to standing still

In the photographs of the station.

■

While cinders are blazing
The smart woman never lives in one house

She steps down from the train
A polyester dream in the rush,
Commuters swirling all around her

He reflected on the several items
The 1974 Plymouth revolving
Catches her light on a fender

She flings her totebag over her shoulder

At the news stand buying a NEWSWEEK
The change in a white hand
Quarters attempt to reflect him

Good

Since there's nothing sterling
About him. She vanishes in the crowd
He chooses his thoughts carefully
aloud

■

Photographs!

Some happily sing
They have joy for white shirts
Singing "O white shirt!"
And that's just the start

Their love of the subject
Continues and it grows
From Jacques Lartigue
The poetry the cruelty of flight
To Alfred Stieglitz baby pictures
Of pollution becoming disaster

Headlines POLLUTION BECOMING

No no no don't torture me *this* way

DISASTER. Thanks, now we can
Take the paper with us to Bklyn.
The Plymouth admits its emissions
How to avoid other sins?

■

I can smell the gauge. The confusion
Is like a cloud swirling before you
Proud of making you seem so regal and
So on

She walks the liberated walk

■

A man crashes with his shadow.

In the glass of the train a commuter
Reads a newspaper under his shoulder

■

The photographic room records the history
Of I times
The camera is painted white
Bright colored rugs on the carpet

Shall I sleep now & wake
To sing these songs for you,
my dearest

I'm sorry to have been such a fool

Your costume was much better;
Noticed that the day we met
Walking around that day, we choose today
& somehow some better circumstances

A man crashes with his shadow

I'd like to check your influence
Over these ordinarily mysterious things
Perhaps you are the responsible one!

■

So now you have announced again your power

What now?
Shall we pretend to play stars? Shall
We act the burn out strivers
Or just that the costumes are
Getting better. Better than us!

■

Well, better them than us or I!

■

You do not sing this song to me
nor say it;

We cannot even think
What song to sing
After someone has threatened
"The truth" and someone else

Someone else reports how tired at last
From people misusing the name

That is why we few have surrendered.

■

Soupault's thoughts like coupons
Suddenly turn up on the pages
Your favorite general magazine

The heart goes through its paces
Like a white stallion

■

It takes one day more to spoil the elephant

Recognition leaves
A sailor's silhouette book
Get back, Jo-jo!

Alternatives wake like the first tide
Like light thrown from the blades of a fan
An uneducated war settles for being a cow.

When a war has become merely a cow
The consequence in each finds his turn.
Regular work tires the women, but not
the night men. It's becoming a scandal

If it's peace you want keep your ears open
To women's proposals

But keep your eyes open too

■

> *Un homme tombe avec son ombre.*
> *—Sessutu proverb*

A man crashes with his shadow

He remembered all of this. And now
Seeing her alight from the train,
Suddenly he could understand everything!

But he couldn't remember its name

As he disembarks from the train
He walks promptly into a photograph's
Finish. That's just how slick he is

■

THE TWENTIETH CENTURY

As air brakes shush her
On the tracks
His reflections returned
To those monuments:

The Rye Chair with frayed canvas
Marked RYE, N. Y. 1956

Sit around drinking beer

The mountain with four mugs carved in it
Called "Mugging Mountain" on postcards

Cameras closing in for the credits

■

Rotten car.

■

Remember the night and the TV light and the music
Neon extravaganzas over the rush

Stilled in the photographs of the station

The stillness surrounds the sleeping commuter

The silence salutes those who have crashed

■

Deaf dogs make poor bellhops
The hand's palm deceives no one
Especially if the no ones are
Gypsies. Unless they are businessmen

Those who want to be fooled
See an oasis. Across the desert

Merchants more foolish

Desire is a snowscape on a placemat
Currier & Ives

■

When the microsecond of repose
Finally comes to you you repose
In a beautiful family room

The lovely family gathers
Around the radio's peak
All of them wearing suspenders
Listening to postwar NEWS

Worried about Weingarten's meat prices

Breathing air peaceful and deep
The TV set's soundtrack lightning
A pretty face on the horror movie
Soothing and handsome to their eyes

SUICIDE ADMINISTRATION

homage to Pablo Neruda

We are keeping your file on the desk

The pink paper label NERUDA
Against the manila folder
A painted bathing beauty smile

Another file on a desk smiles ALLENDE

A memo blank
Clipped on the front
Says "Shot himself

Several times in the back . . ."

Here, at the Suicide Administration
We are overworked but efficient

We are only doing our jobs. We have no blood
On our hands

But these files
Remain on our desks

Gentlemen:
Please forward your last letters.
Then we can close these files

ANCIENT HABITS OR CUSTOMS

A hurricane is swirling in the gulf
You can see it in the paleness of the sky

Electric pointillism slowly forms
A colorfully indecipherable maze
And boisterous ecstatic recitations
Flood the loom

A rendering of human form appears

A peasant ignorantly gazing at the sky
Which, even then, is filled with clouds
Floating like trash in a vacation lake

■

He is slowly chipping memories
From space. Something remembered

That cloud looks like
A crumpled phone bill

An old woman
Sidesaddle on a giraffe

An atom bomb

■

Way in the distance, villagers mad with loyalty
Complete with struggling young girls
Prepare to make their stupid sacrifice

Inhuman homage! Loathesome celebration!

Huge boredom is their gruesome gift
To Coaxialcable, the greedy god
Worshipped in this part of Mexico

MOUTHOLOGY

James *I, xxvi–xxvii*

Say justice speaks so
Calmly in your afternoons
A Chinese quiet floods
Your usual square concerns

You read your Bible
So

The wooden garden on your desk
Softens into the Light

Dramatically filtered through venetian blinds

Say justice speaks so
You say you have given

Dinner invitations to the hungry
Hand-me-down clothes to the poor

Even the stars have opinions

Admit to defense it's more blessed to give
Blushes to streakers
                    gone mad
Behind their relatives'
                    freedom

Say noonday finds you walking
Walking on the Kings Highway
Miscegenation seems to you alone
A blessing in disguise

So!

In the light of your own testimony
We has carefully considered your case:
1966 came & went and still
You did not want to be a liar

You

You memorized the stars in their places
For each afternoon
You have made mention

You have visited the VA Hospital
And cheered our boys

Widows have wept at midnight
for your smile

You've even made martinis
                                        at midnight

So now yours is the Kingdom

Come come

HURRICANE DORIS

The trees are loud;
The forest, rooted, tosses in her bonds
And strains against the cloud.
—Alice Meynell

Our pleasure now
Is an efficient squalor
Alternate use of bed
And car. We live in shifts
Of anger and distrust

There's a sock in the kitchen
A book & a comb on the floor
Phone numbers under the bed
Candy wrappers wrinkled on the chessboard
A Scott towel beside the TV set

Soup in my hair
My favorite imported beer (warm)
A warm domestic chaos
Spells life without care
People who could care less

About the other one (though caring)
A painful disappointment
Gathers like a stuffy nose
battling the arms of meditation

Unclear devices
A sense that even silent hurt
Is quite a victory
Over (another) possible disaster

No lucky stars find welcome in our thanks
Which mask disgusted eyes
With dark infinities of manners
Childhood ideas of politeness

A signal sine wave mayday in a glance

But the Carla or Edith in my heart
Is not polite. With a calm eye
She sends her rages flooding to my brain

My own (mild) care numbs speech
Rehearsed in silence
At this point, I can put
A record on the box
Without caring what music

What music can comfort me now

The other woman that is the hurricane
Of everything I must have wanted
In you,

Look how even if she recedes from my heart
She wastes in this house

Look
Leaving heaps of me and mounds
Of you unshapely and deplored
By our own eyes

You can see the false rendering
Fine as the fax lines
Of the disaster wirefotos
Or the minutiae of our
Less than tropic furies

What music can comfort me now I'm mad

            I'm mad
I'm mad because 1,000s of poor peoples
Don't have nowhere to go

Because I must rush to the rooftop
To despair or await you

The disorder of our living
Strangles my peace when you're here
And when you've gone the somewhere
I have no idea, I use no lights
I close the blinds the house turns dark as night

I would rather not see that you are absent

Yes. I'd make a lopsided correspondent

I'd prefer your passion in detail
To the awesome task of cleaning up

EVRY MAE

She contends with clouds of fortune
When she wants

tsk tsk

Does not ask
since it will not be given

Been taught to work for what she needs
Been taught to suffer silent griefs alone

Her few ideas of comfort
Sunlit dusk and modest warmth

Grandmother living room
Couches with claws
In stuffy somnolence
Beneath the icons of the poor

Pictures of Lincoln   Kennedy
Jesus praying at Gethsemane
Martin Luther King at pious best
And Jimi Hendrix
hair bubbling schizophrenically
into a burning bush

Yes. But her dream is Essence
And a shiny face

The flowers shyly fend
against pollution

The mocking season waits

Deco cowboy printed flowers
on her shirt

Her dream is Essence
and a shiny face

SPRUCING SPRING UP ON LARKIN STREET

I want to get up and do
something but I guess someone
already has

She's pushing that
that that lawnmower
but I can't see the lawn
from this angle

Elm trees shape sunlight lozenges
on the brown siding
as other music waits:

Serena Shaw singing IT'S A LAZY AFTERNOON

The shift whistle at Burlington

Children whispering giggles

The tractor man walks
back and   forth
                        around
his complicated sputter shop
                    until she turns
over

But by that time that
that that lawnmower lady,

        she's finished with the invisible lawn
and out of the Arkansas sky
pale and blue as a dirty mirror

a green song comes up sprucing up
the spring

ANOTHER POEM IN ENGLISH

John Donne would think of an island
After all this noon is written
All afternoon I think of several
Words

change   ribbet   foment   format

Plan   plane   solder   alchemy   Army

leads   you're kidding   gaoled

Corsica   desire   solidarity

insular front   font   Louisiana   Rumania

Roumania

The execution of light

Known also as peace about being
A serpent twines itself around space
Wanting to call this that. Really

I'm doing that anyway!
Anyway, I'm doing that

And this this

Jambalaya

RHUMBA NEGRO

This I have told you before

Downtown east your own sky
Green as the oceans you came from
The rhumba negroes are
Hypnotizing the pigeons

Messenger   messenger
        Wash their eyes
Flash like snow in the eyes
        Of the deep witness
New Year we have made
        Our keepsake fearing
Its impression it make
        On our souls.

We are bad men on the street
                                        inside

Your mother and invisible sisters
Static from your radio thought
It was very late in the evening

Kerchief in my hand heart on my sleeve

Europe snows where my arms
Lift without muscles

I wear a blunt white village
Talents on my wrist
When it hears the orisa
It cannot keep the time

FALSE ALARM

The Martians scowl from their gleaming
Machine

The street is quiet. They
Had thought they were taking
Their lives in their hands

They flash and wail back across town
Back to the boring Fire Station

Near the callbox
On the corner
Esu laughs into the night

He laughs until his eyes shine
Bright as the red globe
Blushing up above   his head

Then he gets on his bicycle and
Marches away through the air

R & B

Night just keeps on arriving
Crossing its legs
Waiting for daylight

The old songs flash
Into the radio out of
An electrical night

As for you you have a fool
Like me

THE ARCHITECTURE OF DEVOTION

At the doorway of Anderson Hall
He stands with a large folder
Containing happy schematics for the capital
Letter "I" and blueprints for flowers

SAINT

O excellent night
She move the veil from my eye
Dig. In the dark night
The shaduf is a lamp
Beautiful to the nations
And the boats glitters
Up in the clouds. Yes it is.
Come on in spirit
Make us to understand
All praise to the wit of the
Winds

O excellent night
And my journey commences
I am taken from the lip
Of the waters, planting a tree for a lamp in a dark country
As the pearls on heaven's dark breast
The boats returning
From the seminal nation
The flood bursting
Beneath them, a lamp
Swinging in the far distance
Horizon

In this day

O excellent night
Confused as a bird in the dust storm

Etherized beatification
I am alone on this bridge
And the dark waters below me

In a dim room I am remembered when the lamp is relighted
And the ink suggests corruptions to the page

From the far wall there is sound
To amuse me. There is music
I am alone on the bridge and fire surround me
Barefoot in my chair beneath an atheist's
Likeness. Vehement in guilt with a necklace
For comfort
For neighbors I copy a clef
In the hymnal

I cheat. When I walk through the southland
Dressed up like a blind negro
Stocking cap on my head my skullcap
In glory and my mendicant's tin cup

And 12-string pawnshop steel guitar and white smile

You can say that I stood on the hill
Of our Savior

Lord and I looked down on the house where I used to live

And the rivers of fire and oceans afire
Bright sky turning cloudy

Bright sky turning cloudy
From the white man's Damballah
Backed back to the wall Lord
Minutes cut from yr wrist Lord
O ignorant night
Stamps for the righteous
Seals for the loyal

Thin shoes for sinners

Gold cups for the merciful a jukebox for the lustful
And the ones on the backseat

Hear who say selah

In the glorious dawning I lifted my shoulder
And earned the north window
And the feasts on the greensward
And the rings of the riot

WITCHES

Keep it up. Hear
Everything is right and

In the future when gangster movies
are shown on the thermograph
We still think of the first days
And the mystery of 6s and lights

Drawn from the body
And other sciences
We were confounding ourselves
And ideas intruding on
Revelation and uproar

Accept it as an eon's entertainment
Or Karma

Waiting for the calibration of unnecessary
Emotions

In the future when hard sex pictures
Are shown on the thermograph
We still think of the first days

Wondering why this solitude has drained
nothing from nothing

As when you touch her
Beams contend with the glass
In her hand
Though the words in her mouth
Are so cold. Wanting you
to say you will stay as
You turn round and do stay
Digging her signals

Like she was more than she is
Which is something
More than herself
Like a spirit to be discovered lately
In a neglected old song
Something she would
Like. You imagine
You could care less

Stop and think about her and the time and soft
Light

Like she was more than she is
And had power beside you.

Like she was more than a future

HIGH HEEL JESUS

And

I just can't understand
Some of you people talking
About Jesus

You stupid. Mess over your
Neighbor think you doing
Right right

No you not right doing that
Jesus

My woman hates to see me in my form
Of wisdom madness greed and ghetto
Charm. And I hates to see her go out

Twilight every night
But it's about the rent

You know we has to pay the rent

COLLECTIVE POEMS

for Ishmael Reed

I gather light

Rich white men collect money or stamps
But the poor can't afford that.

I have been a collector
Of tones, a sound keeper
Lifting words from thin
Anguished American timbre
Pitching them in my bin.

Documenting and mending
Adding colored nuances
Collected "dusk" and made it sing
In my album, "chicken" dances

Though before it flinched & cried
And sank out of sight like any
Old poor black man wretched and denied.
But my collection enhanced it.

Of course, I've changed my "luck" and made "power"
Flourish in common places

I brought back "John" from an island
In Florida. I collected "trash" and
Added antique connotations;
Changed all the understanding
Of them who dig my collection.

Made like I tolerated antagonism
Only to uplift the defamed
My people sing and dance it
I made "bards" of my excluded brothers
When the bigots refused me my name.

Been so poor, but a magnet with my shamed English

I have reclaimed the Legends

SPIRITUAL

for Thi Mon

Khi nao troi mua
O phurong nam
Cac cay lua theo mua
Nhu tim cua toi
Theo chi-oi . . .

I feel just
Like my Jesus
Must have felt
Three days past life
& the shape
Of suffering
Still on him
And obvious
To his doubtful friends.
Immaculate
Invisible
To the one
Stoned on the shame
Of doubting or denying
Him   when He was
Here

You knows my name
You know who side I'm on

I feels
As how his mother
Had to feel
So sad
Now say, I gots to go
And leave you dear
And break
His mother heart

I feel that bad
To be alone tonight

One me here now and
Mysteries of the lamp
If my lamp have gone out
Who is shining?
If these thoughts is evil
What

Of evil I ask why
White boys must roam de world
And call old men in short pants
Out their name
As black as me, I wonder
And "aware"
Have I a share on this, my little store
Of pride and wants
Part of that shame

But in this night
I almost don't even care

Since you have gone
I am not even here

If my lamp have gone out
Who is shining

I'm so far beyond living
I make light

Conversation
With the stars
As they arising

I wander unseen
Through your world

All I say is thank you
Jesus, I loved this girl

Khanh Hoi, Saigon, 1971

HOUSE OF RED LIGHTS

Oh

The wind began to whistle
And trees began to howl
The rage of night was coming
As the sun was going down

I was sitting in a dark room
Pictures of you were on my mind

But that just enlarged my sorrow
Just to have you on my mind

It could be worse than better
Since you introduced me to the Blues
I could be sitting on the corner
Earning a doctorate in booze and

Paying all kinds of dues. So it ain't
That bad, even though it's bad for me
No it ain't that bad even though it's bad
for me

I just sit here and I worry
Where on Earth the girl can be

I see a window lighted red
Red as wine wept whiskey eyes
A blue sky filled with stars

Filled with crowded midnight
Signs

Where can she be? I think I can remember
Way back in the country
On a day that's browned and gone

I used to sit and hold your hand
Hoping your child would favor me:

I used to sit and play my harp
Yearning to be a singer with the band
Just look what you did to me:

When I was freezing in Korea
You were down in New Orleans
But the only thing I wondered
What did I do to make you mean
So much to me

When I got back from Seattle I searched for you
All over town

When I got back from Seattle I searched for you
All over town. By the time I found you
I'd just heard you put me down. Girl,

I done everything possible for a man to do

I went along with the street
For about sixteen Bars
Learning to be a singer
With the band.

The wind scaled its floating holler
Pine trees fiddled off a tune
As the rising of the planets
Scored the universe for June

Where the Milky Way across the sky looked like a razor scar
I saw red light from planet Mars winking ON and OFF afar

Oh

I saw a window lighted red
As the path a bullet flies
A blue sky filled with stars
Like salts developing snapshots
Gatherings of midnight sighs

I found her in a dark dark room
In a house of red lights

And I caught her in a lasting pose

And the judge he give me "life"

SOUNDS OF JOY

The firmament of my dungeon
Shakes. And I recline back
Into my dramatics of darkness
And doubts of reaching a night

Where there is nothing
But light. And I imagine
That stars beg my love
In her same soft tongue

The firmament of my dungeon
Shivering like a dancer
The fastness of my steps
Roundward and upward
The foundations of the split
And slide. Over the sand,
Hieroglyph secret sign
The ceil of the wishing
And sealings of my prison
I felt the caulkings of my dungeon
Shake and felt that
I too was a star who fell
From the blue sky of my cell
That loved me. My breath
Warmed her soft belly and
I lay on her heart. Soft
Like a feather. My sister,
Silences of Shango. I mean
The pulses of your soft neck
A thunderous mime of the cosmos
Exclaiming its laws
Musical and luminous
The whole band down on their knees
And the eye in your eye

Bright in the soft baby spot
As you pulse near your ears
In your wrists I hold lightly
With my fingers. In your thigh
Touching my thigh. Your instep
Of your light feet dancing
Across mine. And your neck
Drumming lightly into my ear.
I heard my dungeon tremble and
Felt like my time-house shake. And
The silences of the discovered
Knot-people at their party
Please. Steam of sweat rises up
Soft and dark. South of the heart
Lungs expand wings and suddenly float
Through the nearness of luscious skies

New Black music. Light. The loss
Of the cosmos. Bending sss
Slipping they spine. Wiggle their
Heads hands up cupped to fists
For the moment to kick the guitars
Into two note one riff substantial
Orbit. Fire and Water. A poor man's
Heartbreak. I see the light
Spinning around you
Through my jail windows. Ice
hearts. I touch your black
Nipples ringed with stars
Like any cheap dancing girl
But they really are stars and
Lord lady my dungeon shakes!
Your thigh shining like the desert dark
In the night full moon after flood
The water transmitting your name
From the black antennas of hair
Standing up for the music we make

From an astral dream
I hear the charge in the chests of invisible drummers
Telling rhymed lies in your blood
And the singer steps forth in your
Eyes wearing an aluminum dashiki
And purple bush in the cabaret light
Day creeping in your blinds
As my heart rolls down in the dirt
And my arms scream like young horny
Schoolgirls. The lymph in my body
Counterfeits knots from the terrible
Priest books. Unravel. Knot again.
My sperm bang their heads on the wall
Of their subway like commuters
Going mad with the current events
Of superior worlds they cannot
Know anything more about the tortures
They have been trained up to desire.
My sister. My fingers ruffle the small
Snake coiled above your behind

As kingly manikins might jerk their wands
The cobra wakes and strikes. My sister.
As Erzulie climbs out of her glass. Might
Move to speak. Sout. Sout. As Isis later.

Sasa. Sasa. As the knot complains in her
Throat where the pulse lay the duppies
Our sad Christian yearnings birthing our
Ancient dark African self. Sa. Sa. Sout

As she fights me and my temple breaks
She slays me. Dancing. And I slake my heart
With the mist of her hiss in her mirror
And I rest in the dark hold of her eyes.

And the lines of my vocal extend. The hand
moves further from the skin. The strings.
And returns less often to caress her. And
My dungeon trembles. And my body shakes.

Please. Whosoever our motions may please as we are pleased
In the ocean of our mad moment
And I am tied up in the knot of her
Escape from being an earth girl.

She becomes heaven more than stars. And stars
Of our children glisten in the dark oasis
Marked by her tangled hair. She calls me Kush,
A star in our bodies' tears in her hair

This is our mother. Her dark soft face
Shines beneath hair plaited like palmtrees
Forever and ever and ever. She touch me.
She call me by our father's name because she

Mean she loves me. She says. Shh.
Her white teeth glint in the dark sky
Of her soft heavy lips. They are like
Stars trying to learn how to dance

THEY'LL BE BACK

Morning morning Sunday
In my own backyard
A squirrel took over
My backyard for Spring!

A squirrel!

Four corners. Barking coughing
At the squirrel world. And me.

A cat a tom sings nightly
By the door.
I can't go out

In side I listen to some records from LA

A deep successful brother in the Bar
Says "Bird Coltrane Eric Dolphy man

What if they had lived!"

LE ZODICO NE PAS SEUL

à Clifton Chenier

Avoir douleur mon coeur
Pain in my heart. Chagrin
I love her so

She tears when she cry
Tears was even sweet

You know
You never miss salt water
Until the late night rains
The lightning flash

Between the clouds & her reflection
Vanish from my window-pane

■

Across into the trees I see
The sky turn white with rain
These clouds be with me, I am not
Alone. Clouds says to me: —

Avoir douleur mon coeur

Please don't antagonize your spirits
Don't advertise your mind.

Even she never come back to you
You not alone

Avoir douleur mon coeur
She also sings to you

JUBILEE

from the Egyptian

O Sun!

Both halves of the country
Adore Thee

O Sun!
The whites prostrate themselves
Seeking color
Our people bow
To hear the famous songs
They praise you up
At your rising
Your body revealed
Dazzling the land

Your day-clothes shed
Beautiful light!

We know you in your garment

Your loud colors make the young brothers laugh
That's a young man's shyness and praise

They slap hands in admiration, touching
The palms you have made golden forever
Dancing slyly in amusement for you, O Sun

Sun.

Our ancestors called your name
Before they called us the names
We are called

We are out of Egypt
Ethiopians
We stretch forth our hands
Just as in the ancient

Holy sign
We sing
We scat do do do do do it
That is adoration
It is never enough

But we praise Thee
With all the love
We can bear being modest
And meek
Desiring most your presence
And care we adore Thee
In our own night we fear
Ignorantly

But you always return.

Out of the womb of our Mother endlessly
You appear. In your boat at the dawn
At your station sailing into the West

What a long watch! Long as the patient care
Of young women seeing you sailing
Still patient until you return. That's
Adoration

Our ancestors called your name
In their own youth
Beyond many millions
Of days. They would
Stop weeping to sing it
Though they had
As many reasons for
Sorrow. And as many
Lost names

All the members of higher planes too.
Sing it's a new day

The great armed ones adore Thee
The little ones shouting and shaking hands
Adore Thee in your beautiful aura

The poem "Jubilee" is translated from the hieroglyphic hymn to Ra from the door jamb of the tomb of Horemhab, general and later Pharaoh at the end of the XVIII Dynasty. The hieroglyphs are reproduced in A. H. Gardiner, *Egyptian Grammar* (Oxford: Oxford University Press, 1973), 291–92.

♍

I have Roy Ayers on the box my sunny time
And three Hebrew Angels
Bearing the Sign out the East

Zubulen, Rachael & Azamatafach

Sound Science

A NATIVE GUIDE

Correct principles can move
Mountains. And build worlds. Far out
In space. This is all truth
With one word you set me afire

PYRAMIDS

With one word you set me aflame
I am saying the word. The word
The syllables that sing your name
You have me burning like a sun

THE NEW BORNING

You have this world and others
All just spinning around me

MORE THAN NOTHING

You have given me new sights of the skies
And taught me that we are the wholes in space

THE PERSUADER

You are my sweet professor

A JUDGE

Since you are my lover I have
Everything coming to me. But
Yesterday my everything seemed
Like it was not quite enough

DUDS

With one word you just put me on flame
How can anything from me be enough?

MY CALLING

When I call you. Or your name
I want a saxophone player to play
Because as I say I love you
That "you" makes me blaze.

THE OFFERING

You deserve a sonorous kiss
A bright polished bell of brass
An offering to the you
I adore. Or I need a pianist

SPEAK LOW

I want some music for you.

LOW SPEECH

That will not make these lyrics more beautiful

O my pitiful songs!

Can't you take her sounds
Extravagant sounds
Beautiful as the sound
Of her name? Huh songs?

Take to her gleaming planets
And exuberant stars.

ARC IN THE DARK

The song light sparkles
In my eyes. My eyes
Grow darker and deeper
Just like deep Space
And my pitiful songs.

MAGNETISM

We are traveling to and forth on the sound
Going and moving and coming
That is the science of sounds
Said with love. Heard with care
That is me saying and singing

O the beautiful coils of your name!

Ssss

THE UNIVERSE

What shines is your black body
This is all truth. Reflected
In the dark space of my dark eyes

Or can it be the lighting in the room?

And thunder. If thunder says
"Listen, I am the Thunder.
I am the Solomon of a small space
And a sun blazing"

This is a hieroglyph.

THERE'S A LOT OF WISDOM HERE

There's a lot of the Wisdom here. See that

ONE MORE CHANCE

When you are alive
You'll love my songs

Songs for people being born
(signed) Lorenzo

WHAT I WOULD PREFER

I'd prefer music for you.

WE ARE BEAUTIFUL AFRICAN PEOPLE

On the count of one, drums will clatter like rain
On two, the hills
Will rumble out their gladness
The joy of my shout returning
As my voice fondly plays your name
Without music it sounds so strange

PROTECTION

Sometimes I'm saying I love you
Those words in English mean
I will not let anyone hurt you
But me

That all.

POSSESSION

Love I am all despair in my language
Even though you are making me a sun
Out of ancient sound science,
I am calling you or your name

OBEDIENCE

je t'aime

OIL OF GLADNESS

I am trying to make my songs
More beautiful still. Still
I'd prefer music to give you

Chances Are Few

MY OFFICE

I've spent the last 10 years
In other people's offices
Learning the alphabet of nods and eyebrows
And pursed lips, straining for the purse
Legs crossed in easy confidence
Confident nervous gestures of assurance
Approved blue suits
And sudden dreamed-up lies to be delivered

A net of thirty days and sixty days and ninety
Insanely stretched past promise into years
Next week, for certain
Floated haphazardly on possibles
As slight as handshakes,
Firm as agreements of subjective verbs

And got nowhere.

This happy corner, sucking up hard-boiled eggs
And Polish hots
The seidel sliding down the polished bar
Clatter of friendly pool balls in the margin
Not exactly somewhere, but a certain place.

A regular's dark hair and polished eyes
Glow in the glasses lined before her face
Smoking and berating the muzak
"Jack, when you gonna get some country music?"

"Country Charlie Pride?"

Outside, it's as bright as the important phone call
I always pretend to await
Setting up the lunch meeting at Stouffer's
Linen napkins and hope's frozen green peas

Set up another round of handshake laughter for the pictures

"Hey sweet thing, when we gonna have that date?"
The barmaid pouts a 1940s frown—
It's Arnie (reaching now to slap me on the back)
A gleaming brazen polyester clown,
Tuesday seems longer than the day before
Since I began to organize my life around My Office
I stay a little later every day.
A little rain hangs fire in the clouds

Next trip, I think I'll bring the wife

I

The Fine Clothes of Year before Last

No one
has ever
given me
an even break
but God
—Percy Mayfield

INAUGURATION

The land was there before us
Was the land. Then things
Began happening fast. Because
The bombs us have always work
Sometimes it makes me think
God must be one of us. Because
Us has saved the world. Us gave it
A particular set of regulations
Based on 1) undisputable acumen.
2) carnivorous fortunes, delicately
Referred to here as "bull market"
And (of course) other irrational factors
Deadly smoke thick over the icecaps,
Our man in Saigon   Lima   Tokyo   etc   etc

THE FINE CLOTHES OF YEAR BEFORE LAST

Only fit now
For the garden, the carwash,
The ritual of stinking for four days
To solve a problem
That stinks to you to high heaven
And just in general stinks

Sweating and sleeping
In these shabby clothes
An almost Biblical humility

Remember the pretensions of these slacks
Outmoded now by cuffs
That once were fashionable
Now only blows to style's ego

The shirt's stiff vanity
Long ago frayed into a makeshift coverup
For Saturday mornings' inopportune doorbells
That scheme to steal the self-bestowed rewards
Of a week's toil and Friday night good fortune
A shirt so homely and contrite,
Those days were brave. The only peals
It dares to answer lately are the phone's.
Original function almost completely faded from memory
Superseded by last month's soft stars:
The sad blue one featuring Bette Midler's lips
The dashing gold with Mondrian motifs
Haughtily synthetic carefree exaggerations,
slouching on hangers,
These treasure their trips to the cleaners
Like sad husbands playing at wit in distant cities
Like old fools with young girls anywhere at all
While old stud gets funky
And goes straight through the wringer

With rags, dirty drawers and soiled linen.
One with experience,
No novelties or mysteries remain ahead.
No mystique remaining.
So agitated and spun by lifelong turnings, even the bones
Would be lost long ago if they weren't stitched in.

This shirt feels softer than the world it once confronted,
Suitable now only for faceless moods
        That's the necessity that summons all
Things
        The only reason they are still around
Perhaps

        That
Someday
        They shall be useful beyond purpose

The matching tie, though, is still splendid
Still wide in vogue
Living in the glove compartment
An emergency cravat.
It has folded itself into this honor
Its true office diminished
By the fate of its shirt

FARTING AS DECENCY

à John Berryman

Someone essays the ultimate step
Which illuminated the late news
And gives us something odd to relate
To the next afternoon at the Club.

When you die, of course, you will abhor
Any reference to yourself over a beer
Or tom collins. You will appreciate any
Respite in a drunkard's consideration

Of you and your first wife. Your departing
This life of toil, manners and strife.
You'll appreciate any skip in the record
Of your descent. The bar maid's fart.

SECURITY

No headaches or heartaches
Or misunderstands . . .
—Thomas A. Dorsey

All Americans are losing
Their minds are going crazy
With the fear of being
Alone
In the world
Going nowhere

The air marshals of the future
Search everyone at the gate

Americans must go nowhere
—THE DIRECTOR

On the bulletin board

This is undisguised information
Nothing covert no leaks no culvert
& no Calvert

I declare!

The speaker
Announced no changes of seaport
The move is to be made by air

No charts. Somehow they'll get there
That's what all the bon voyageurs share
That simple hope waving their hankies

All Americans are going going
"Those honkies!" hissed
The protestants at the pier

And "I, too, am an American"
Dreamed a lovely desirable gone white girl
Marvelously sedated in a chair

PERSONAL ANTHROPOLOGY

How abject beauty are
Our own reflections
They show so little of us

Our syllables dwindle in this beauty
Like colors in shadows of turrets
Walls
Selfish determinations
As we transfer our pain
To a Monet a pattern of colors
Seurat and pointed lines

In our small rooms in fronds of TV sets
We become pointillistes of conversation

Our own problems grow
No larger
As we quietly sit
Amused by the fun
Watching several deranged little people
Tormented in a box on the table

Total boredom's majesty
We forge a newer Milarepa learning

Suffering proudly and silent
Bravely at bedtime
Absorbing the shocks
Of the news. Sadnesses
And policies doomed
At last, compassion for a President
Poor Gerald Ford

BROADWAY–LAFAYETTE ESPADRILLE

DIARY OF A SOLDIER

6th Avenue. 28th Street.
The green bus appeared
Headed uptown. Determined.

Full of rabbis with earlocks
And beards. Backwardly
Thumbing their books
Past the towering greed
Each deliberate corner
Halting their speed
Toward a promised appearance
Somewhere uptown I guess

POPULAR FORCES

Hum, said a beautiful sister
Glad I'm not a Jew

WRONG FACE HUH

I think I understand how she felt
Not really understanding I guess
Grown men with beards on the shule bus
Collecting ignorant comments
Imperturbably headed uptown

But then, what could you tell her?
Count neckties in the Subway?

BRIEFING

The ignorance of appearance
Holding everyone back
Or the ignorant traffic

THE RIGHT FACE

Bring

I hear the second alarm. I leap and
Shrug on my sneakers and dash
To the front of the shape up
Prepared check ready check do it
Check. I load my Malcolm X book
In my back pocket for lunchtime

A MESSENGER (MY SLAVE)

A good job. I go sweeping through
The City machinegunning the buildings
My eyeballs red from so many
Rounds. With my satchel under my arm
Walking into the lobbies and freight
Doors in the immaculate fronts
Of the City's tawdry business
And the words coded between each
End of a luncheonette counter

CONTACT REPORT

Too much reefer this morning. Too much wine last night?

FORWARD

The Broadway number jumbled up in my brain
My mind's dream of Walt Frazier
And/or Black Revolution. And *rifa*
All down to my feet moving swift

In my sneakers. Is this the wrong Broadway?

Swoop back downtown. The same burthen
Too much reefer
On my head back and forward
Through the City all day

THROUGH THE NEEDLE'S EYE

Carrying Seventh Avenue dresses
Packages of careless fortune
For the Man for the ignorant
Beautiful sisters buying
This garbage sale day
At Ohrbach's for nearsighted Jews
And yenta daughters in law
From Lack Success and Ft Lee
New Jersey. Back downtown down
Through Hell's Half-Acre back
Now to Broadway and Lafayette
And its alarming psycho-sexual
Capitalist charm

PRESENT ARMS

Long silken hair big leg Puerto Rican ladies of sensuous
Armpits.

Rap to this one
    Hey *¡corazon!*

I got *azucar pa ti*

Dig? *Me el mensajero*

You dig? She frown
And is gone down
The busy street and
I wonder what it is
Or where it is

And I wonder just where
In Hell I am. Dammit,

I'm lost

ATTENTION

A white woman with flat feet
Looks out of her window
She looks oddly at me off
The rim of her eyeglasses

My Malcolm X book in my pocket

Eyes slitted standing here lost like a fool
On the most businesslike wrong corner
In the currency world of our days. Man.

I'm attracting all this attention?

PARADE REST

A bundle of dresses with no woman smell yet
On my head
My two dreaming feet
On the ground

EUCHRE BRIDGE

Allow the prophets to hold the Eucharist as they will
—Didache, *10:7*

Grateful,
I sit and watch
This yellow butterfly
Dip into Chinese tallow

I watched the lowest leaves
Turn orange and then red

They vanished then
Too stylish for the tree

Went off to the city & lights

Now there's about a dozen red leaves
                                        higher up
A yellow butterfly plays
All around them, tempted

Goes off in search of true flowers
Dummy!
        At this late date
It gets early
        Darker than it used to
Poor butterfly

WHEELING

for Clement & Lewis

So

That's redneck music man just wait
You awake just in time
To see the next exit
And remark similar signs

You have seen somewhere
Before. This awakens
The driver and evoked

Gratitude from the death seat
Where I been riding
Alone with the bland view
Of the landscape of that
Highway so like any other
And so dull

That is, lacking the remarks of the roadmaps
Annotating and expanding
As our landmark
The beautiful mountains add
Defiance or yearning
To the depressed States

As the highway captures our car
Which makes no distinctions
Between mountains and States
That is rightly the work of the maps
Pimping the restrooms we desire

Hush your mouth
Just wake up & yr mouth already!
Welcome back to God's country
Wait. I'm *trying* to find the soul
Plus the tape died

About twenty miles down the road

The batteries couldn't stand
All that ignorance in the air
Plus you were asleep
All the way from Ohio

Get yourself together brother man

Nearing home now. You wake up just in time
Take the wheel

TOO LOUD FOR NAMES

She becomes a sagging bosom
Big behind "movin in
Forty-one years of her
                    movin out
Voluptuous & fine
                    disco lady …"
As beautiful as she has been she is
                    Black and
Fading fast lovely
Before your greedy eyes
                    and shy.

She becomes an academic question
When the band wraps up
                    no rendezvous
Saying "Take care y'hear
                    no voulez vous"
We'll be right here back again
                    no "me & you"
                    tonight
This coming Thursday. "All right!"
At home, the sitter watches Johnny Carson
The kids are wrapped up tight.
Yes, momma loves *them.*

THE RULE OF THUMB

for Ron Padgett

I

Opening a can of Coors
In Tulsa, beneath a full moon
Near the Sun Oil refinery
East of Sun Oil west of the moon
Press press and push, thumb ending
Up in the beer
Shake thumb and lick
Sip

Kinda warm (don't you think)
Stand lookout by the window
All clear sneak to ice machine
I-legal bucket held rushing style

Trip

Run back and rebound
Slide back to room along the Trail of Ice
Slip

Back into the room (careful) and ice the Coors
Make two more forays.

Have used up now nine people's share
But, then, there're 60 vacant rooms here.
Tonight's only Monday
An off day in the motel game
Just like in the life,
Blue Monday Blue Monday
But no heart-rending music
No "Rocks In My Bed"
No call me the Winding Boy Everybody Know
My Name

You know you know you know
You know my name
Look up, the number's
On the bottom of the can

No

Torchy songs sputter down
Smooth as faded denim
Muzak
Annoying ooze into the lobby
As very few people check in.
And even fewer fumble
For American Express cards

And there is none
To remark the clerk's boredom
Just an off day in the motel game
In Tulsa

On edge on the outskirts of town,
Those few behind doors,
Whose windows glow,
Are watching Melissa Manchester
Once again flunk the Memorex test
Wishing they had instead
Gone to Europe for the Silver Jubilee
To buy a cup with the Queen's mug
Upon it (GUARANTEED UNBREAKABLE
MARCA REGISTRADA
NOT AUTHORIZED FOR RADIO BROADCAST)
Touch and go

Hecho en Mexico
Cop and blow
Recycled from obsolete Don Ellis records
b/w *Electric Mexicana Rose*
That, in those days, were "ahead
of their time" —*Billboard*

36⅓ on the A side, 46 rpm
On the flip
Gone to Jackson
Jackson Jacksonville
Bowling Green
Or New Orleans

Gone on to New Orleans
To see the mystic treasures of King Thumb,
Sarcophagus mask hammered of Coors
Cans recycled by superstitious fellahin

In the good old days before Palestinians
Were content to pose with their asses
For roving color photographers
Who, with Christian charity and Hasselblads
Immortalized those ingrates in child Bibles
Ennobling skyjacking heathen souls with captions:
These are, perhaps, the scenes that Jesus saw

Ah, sands of time!
Tan snows of yesteryear!
Deserts of memory shift in our minds
Drip
Through the bottle of the picture tube
Cyrus Vance
Kissinger
When they begin the beguine
As electrons

Under Tulsa's fool moon
In this motel's one room
I'm sitting in, watching TV
Escaped from the frayed Blues in the lobby
Muzak
My mind reminds me
Texarkana and Alphonso Trent
Was Music those days

My mood
Reminds me
Of Ron's "Radio"
Tulsa
1921
The riots "riots"
Instead of the Jazz Age
T for Tulsa
T for Tennessee
Bob Wills for Texas
San Antonio Rose
And all that and
Vo de oh doh

Voodoo   Class of '21

Instead, niggers screaming
No jazz
Houses burning
No shimmy
And T too many white folks dreaming
Freak dreams that could never be.
Ignorance churning
These disasters into the brew
That flows out of the mountains
Where the Arkansas rises

Now, under this moon
As you press press and push
Cut your thumb
On the lip of the press-tab
Opening the swirling seals of King Thumb
Mystic treasures of ancient waltz music

Here's your INSTRUCTIONS:
Cut thumb and suck
You are blood brother now

Blood, brother

Ah ee ah hah
Are these the scenes what Jesus saw
With color prints of Colorado's valley
And chicano workers walking picket lines
Is this what Carter and Carnarvon saw
In cursed relics now touring the land
In Ronald Reagan's real DEATH VALLEY DAYS
Press press and push and millions for that cause
More where that came from
And millions flocking everywhere to view
In New Orleans King Thumb and in Chicago
Uh huh ah yeah
You are blood brother now
To weighted hatreds
Of all the centuries
All the enormities of recent years

Of Coors

. . . .

II

PURIFY   PURIFY   PURIFY

Howling a chant to the full moon in Tulsa,
I see the guests stick their heads out their doors
They gleam in the full moon of Tulsa

The faded Blues unravels in the lobby
An off day in the motel game
The night clerk simply snores

I see a shadow in the moon: Our time is hard
It's hard. But fair. And it is just.

Just T for Tulsa
T for Tennessee
T for you too, brother by me

As the spirits are rising
In the light of the moon
Drink *Miller's* (though it's 30¢ more)

We must cling to our vices to prove we are real
But we must also concern ourselves with the main deal

If you're fat, be forgiven
Drink *Lite*
Drink *Schlitz, Anheuser-Busch, Oly*
Dos Equis , even *Stag* near beer

But first of all
Of all the things to do in Tulsa,

BOYCOTT COORS

II

They Never Lose

They call me Sugar Daddy
I am the softest touch in town.
—Mercy Dee

THE LEOPARD

The eyeballs on her behind are like fire
Leaping and annoying
The space they just passed
Just like fire would do

The ground have no mouth to complain
And the girl is no braver herself

She is beautiful in her spotted
Leopard ensemble. Heartless so

To keep her fashionable in New York
Leopards are dying

Crude comments flutter around her
At lunchtime. She sure look good
She remembers nine banishing speeches

More powerful than this is the seam
Of the leotard under her clothing

Her tail in the leotard is never still
The seam!
She feels it too familiar on her leg
As some crumb says something suggestive

The leopard embracing around her
Is too chic to leap and strike

Her thoughts fall back to last semester's *karate*
Underneath, the leotard crouches up on her thigh
It is waiting for its terrible moment!

THEY NEVER LOSE

after Cranach

I

A woman's sense is not her education
But what escapes from Logic,
Literature, and fads of aim
For security's sake, "set your cap for a doctor"
A dentist. At least, a real estate man.

So girls go daft
With or without education
Thinking up men as special Bargain prizes
That only need a little polishing,

A little work. So, they get married
Then, to sanctify the fact, they must buy something.
Whatever. A major purchase.
In the final showroom, tired of dallying,
"Jew him down" floods to her mind
In half-whispers. Theatrical for days.

You go for that?

Well, Rubens ate it up

Thought he was smart, too
Meddling mythology. I tried to tell him
Cranach tried to complain
About the silly hat, but who
Can tell a real or would-be goddess?

Chattlesome morons call it "human nature"
Popping their eyes at any lisp of news.
But, then again, what else is human nature?

Yeah?
How about him, who sees his dreams
Feel too large for the golden ring
A woman with or without education
Sees him performing in?
His purse knows better even if his heart
Is pumping bleeds of Red Grooms
Lithographs from the spring
Trip to New York City. For the foyer.

II

I feel like I'm knocking on Heaven's door
—Bob Dylan

He sees himself an exile in his flesh
Flitting from place to place to relocate
And earn promotions. Finally to some nondescript Chicago,
An overdone but prim Lake Forest home,
Working till nine to pay the premium on his estate.

Be careful, daughter . . .

When the everyday commuter's
Train of thought
Stops short approaching minute stations
Along the pilgrimage to or from toil
And modest dreams of freedom
Ranking somewhere below wealth
But near to comfort
Where no known drug's peace
Is more inebriating
Than the tiresome but firmly held belief
That pain will vanish in the afternoon,
When thought and music masters noise
As effortless as you please,
Umm hmmm. That's when it crashes!

■

OK, I'd classify that one as a dream
—or a disaster.

Lucky we live down South
Everything is flat around here
Even, they tell me, our pronunciation.
That's why we use these big words
Our betters and the redskins left behind

I mean, like "nigra," "pickaninny," "Tennessee"

■

Just then, it happens.
The boss (who never liked this dude)
Begins to wonder
"Say Jim, you think
You might could handle
Nashville?"

Unseemly pride of Equal Opportunity
The presidency of the local NAACP
Fades into visions of the local Klan
Clumsily setting up a sputtering rood
On your front lawn in Nashville, Tennessee:
That's what you get for your mouth
Saying you love her more than life itself

III

The there it is,
I swear to God

That's when it happens:
Dimly, he wavers
Like TV sets of those too cheap to subscribe to the cable

Who can't afford it because their lives are sad
Because there is some tragedy way back
That kept them pure and poor in quarantines of sense

Quite educational.

That's when he wakes metabolized in sleep
Without her cool, soft hand to soothe his sweat
After the dream that shows in twenty years
His broken body managing the shop in South Dakota

Or, worse than that, consulting in New York
Dodging muggers, while she sits watching *Kojak* in Tulsa
As he frets sitting, lonely in an Oyster Bar
Of some dull town's insipid Marriott
Watching ugly blond waitresses bore him
Finally to the disgraceful confession:

"I've made a complete omelette of my life!"

Or else
She sits complacent in her negligee
Watching soap operas
Chewing and snapping gum to old time movies
Dinah Shore
The $100,000 waste of time
While he swinks on at luncheons, demonstrations,
Conferences, sales meetings, briefings, and arguments,
She sits
Becoming sunlight flatters her awhile
While simple sense tells him that women age
Longer than men, since men have heart attacks
From overwork. And, dammit, he can see it all now!
A sense of time or timing counsels him,
Beware. Women have tricks up their sleeves
Even naked

So, sensible women always understand,
A young man's pride goes on the punctual shelf
Of duty after the first date
Until the crucial moment when he dreams
Again of flirting with himself in his disguises:
Always clean and cool
Single, and, for that reason,
Free to act a fool.

IV

> *Helen dramatized the smallest incidents …*
> *—Anaïs Nin*

Only a foolish child falls to despair.

At this point, woman reaps
The fruit of sisterhood.
People will talk. It does her good to listen
Even if they heap badmouth on her man,
It's good advice, experience, instructions.
You want an apple or a wedding ring?

Paris my foot. The thought! That stuck-up
Sucker

One man, three women
Who he think he is?
One who thinks she's got him
          Even if he strays
One who yearns to keep him
          If he stays
One who feels she's lost him
Still dreams of other days
My dear, it's worth your time to learn
At least those three graces,
And not be caught confused
Between a man's natural two-facedness

Lord, yes! A woman's strength

That leaves
Him, who fears another's feeling,
Defeated finally in merely choosing
Defeated formally in memory's anticipations
Like the last time you thought you saw
Just what you thought you saw
A kind of fleeting shame and frozen sorrow;
Control of nothing left but needless options

But now, the deal was closing in her eyes

TOO MUCH ONE THING, NOT ENOUGH SOMEWHAT ELSE

Progressive Reggae

O brother stay strongest

None but a no good woman tries to fool you
A good one understands it's not her place to rule
You, as equals share
You know what sharing's like:
She'll wake up coughing
In the middle of the night
And ask if *you're* all right

Stay strongest, brother.

Not even necessary to shed a tear;
Just the unstable moisture of confusion only
Condensing
Trembling a strong voice
To catch or whimper
Is enough . . .
The first drop of the torrent and the flood
Not after ever to be denied
(Weakness in a man, brother)
Neither by myth, plain lie,
Historical necessity nor convoluted
Faith

No faith camouflage for weakness
Weathered board and even dumb stone speaks
Even to the most unsophisticated sensors
The high water mark is evidence enough
Visible in your structure of relations

The line that remains gauges weakness
Inadequate plans
Endurance perhaps, like a campaign scar
But strength is not the same thing as endurance
Which speaks to weakness first in private,
Confidently carrying its pleas to higher courts
As the flood rises where the rich folks live.

Each house its own nilometer,
The high water mark is what speaks
Relief for survival, not pride;
Thankfulness for endurance, not praise
Testament to struggle and shameful evidence of weaknesses
Covers every stone on the planet like graffiti
Darkly whistling boasts of terrified Senior Classes
Gone down the drain long ago.
The high water mark is etched in every rock
Humility of uncountable forgotten Pharaohs
Monuments to the weakness of man.

Embarrassment
A bathtub ring coloring our new mutual cleanliness
Trust that!
Experience too clear to be denied
Floating about us, granulated
Dead moons of Saturn
Gleaming and telling. oh brother!

No one, please,
Mishear me. No one
Must take their pleasure in offense
Of what I say to tell my brother
Brother, always stay strongest.
Unless the lamb must be called chauvinist
To fear the shepherd's pie,
This is just an old ram's bleating

Brother, stay strongest always

For even once you fight away the fever
Which comes like a gift with freight charges,
No strength of protest,
Strategy, disgust, or plan …
No plea ever will move
The soft cooling weight of her hand
Loving,
Concerned until governing,
From your brow

You don't need consultations with gypsies,
Bump-readers, or the Corps of Engineers
You just look for the high water sign and the old folks
They will tell you about it
As old Joseph did learn to tell dreams
And the scales at the grain elevator:
Too much one thing, too little somewhat else.

The lines across an old man's forehead
Are lines from a young woman's hand
Imprinted there. It's only natural

She herself old, her palm shines (giving, golden, open)
Smooth as glass.

CHOOSING METALS

This child and the Moon are not speaking.

She has no use for it
If it's not silver. She
Prefers sleep to sunshine.
Her choice of metals
Is a natural

She prefers silver to presents

Her wristwatch and the key are gold-
Colored. She dares not use them

The child never wants milk
On her jello. She cries,
This is too precious for just dessert!

But really it's nothing

GUILT

No longer the feather
She used
To be, her breath still sings

But her head on my pajama sleeve
Is heavy with confused
Determination & vague hurt

My heart
A stone cast in a lake
Catching a sudden freeze
Prisoning the stone
        Half in half out

Rings
Of ice which won't melt

        The rarity of what we've felt
Seems done

In the morning's radiance
When we wake,
She's unsure of my silence
As she chats about the weather

But all I want to talk about
Would be unspeakable things

CANZONE

Strained daybreak breaks in past the blinds
You have your sexy moments with the sluts
And then the sensual response becomes a habit

Birds out of habit utter their sun spells.

Your habit strains
As her delusion finds
Your way to bland
Disgraceful petulances

Blocked. The tape feeds tacit
Arrogance to habit. Madnesses.
The radio announcer's pains
Of authenticity. We understand.

She walks out with Janis Joplin's CHEAP THRILLS

As local "music of the Renaissance" abuts
Her vocal memories of the Shirelles.
O Lord, how vain we are! Ghost music fills

Our Sundays with whatever is at hand
and Idries Shah's THE WISDOM OF THE IDIOTS

SKETCHES OF SUSAN

She tilts her head
To hear the light
Which flows, like her hair
Billows
Turns around
Bob Dylan has it "Bette Davis style"
Hands in
For your gaze's consideration
Hands in her pockets, tilting her head

Now you see her now you don't understand
What you see in her now
A fragment of a simple pose she wears
This one the girl from the plains
This one, the small town aesthete
Her heart in Venice for the Biennale
A debutante refusing to come out.

Now you see her, here, touching a child with glee
And wonder that all Creation exists
Inside the child, inside her caring glance

And now suppose
That she pretends to be a pose a modern woman
Which is completely a shrug
That is, a shrug a long-stepped gait
& a turn (hands in pockets)

Bette Davis style

Mary Cassatt-style, studying the people at large
In their own moments
Painting their postures
But this one, this one who is not Cassatt,
Keeping their eyes to herself

Giving them ordinary representational eyes
Only because portraits have eyes
She gives them eyes, keeping all hope
All sorrow pretense pain all joy and wonder in those gazes
For herself
To still the postures
That those eyes dictate.

She herself poses. Everytime she paints.
And if I were a poet, I'd pose her in two words:
I'd make them up
I'd pose her   that way
And   that way, too

Lithe   gyroscopic

The self-portrait Mary Cassatt somehow just didn't paint

I'd pose her turning
Smiling at the sky
Shaking her hair inside a cotton field

Touching a child with wonder
Like a wand

Being a modern woman as she sees it
Which, really, she (like all of them)
Really don't see. Don't see that our lives
Are mere charades with constant wonder
And surprises we might have seen coming
And got the better of them

But I, like Frank O'Hara, am no painter.
And I fumble to offer no portrait
Just sketches of Susan as sometimes I see her.
In two words, to show what a poor poet I am

Lithe, gyroscopic
Hearing light

Is there some old song that says it? some poem?
Some set of tones that paints a portrait in the light
In the way that light plunges through windows
Into the space of our poses … our bodies styled
In such light as if we were posing the one possible portrait
That impossibly tells all generations "So there!"
Hands in pockets, turning. That's who they were.

She's inside now inside
A room she's made a garden of
Her plants her space her portraits filled with love,
Moving like a diamond stylus
In the song of light which flows
Around & through her
From her hand
Returning to our eyes
The gift of what she sees
So well,
She tilts her head to hear

Portraits have eyes

ELECTRICITY OF BLOSSOMS

for Janet

Plentiful light

Their voices glow in mirror language
A high tension key winding
Brightness called "sky"
These things are atmospheric

Another electricity blossoms
The formal illusionist's hoop

Wireless

          Outside of the daylight
Inside,
   If one could be
   Outside of the light

          The light would appear
From within

Faith

I said, "Little brown electric flower/woman"

Convention

Lady your smile
A shock to my eyes

                    An oriel in a tree

Your concern is the tree

                    Your frown leaves

Plentiful light

Feelings are almost Arabic in this poem

Levitation

My idea blossoms & varies like Light
Embracing light in the glass of a mirror.
A woman. Illusion of someone
Desiring magic tuxedos of mirrors

People who grow closer to surfacing

See stepping out of TG&Y or LEONARD'S

Closer to escaping into day
            trams

HICCUPS

after Leon Damas

Seven gorgeous waters. Gulp!

Three or four times past twenty-four hours
I remember my childhood infancy
In a hiccup sequence

Hiccup hiccup Pope pap hiccup hiccup

Instinct, man . . .

■

My mother gave her son good table manners

■

A fork is not a toothpick!
Don't talk with your mouth
Full of worldviews

When you lift your nose do it right!

Snap beans not salty equals pas sale

Zodico? By all means, no!

Kung Fu fighting no street friends no no
My daddy say let that boy boogie woogie
No no!

A typical West Indian childhood.

And then and then
The Father's name
Of the son

And the holy ghost
Ends in each grace
Fluttering above every meal

Gracc to bc born and transpircd
In every variously memorable dinner pahty

Call it grace

■

Shucks!

■

My mother, Mom
Taught her son memorandums
History lessons in a minor scale
                    on the piano

          Church soup

Yesterday with the yesterday news
          History lessons:

Each child will bear the brunt
Of our Father's name

                    Our Father . . .

■

You you take you
You can't even speak French!
French French
The real French French
French of France
Disaster

I tell myself disaster
Talking to me

My mom taught her son
My mother's son

You have no future salutes
from salesmen

The ones you & I meet
on the street

High or underground Savannah
in the shadow of the Dead's monument

jazz playing

In your "drum battle" with Otis,

Otis
who hasn't even made a comeback
from his
baptism
Can't even speak French dig it?

Disaster
I tell you disaster
I say to myself

■

My Ma
wanted a very do boy
ver-rey very me
very fa no popping off fresh
So
very very
lah de dah, see?
NO HOOKY PLAYING

I remember again it comes to me:
Your *violin* lessons!
A banjo
You say a banjo
How you say it
A banjo you say, "Good … a banjo"

HICCUP!!!

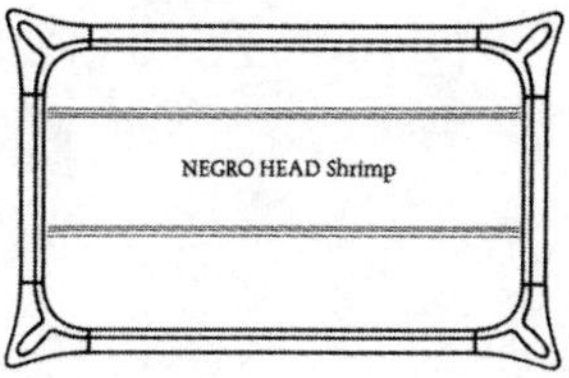

Such labels!

No sir
No siree
No ban
No "Joe"
No "git!"
No tears
No shit
No blues
No more

■

So

    There's no MULATTO water-fountain south of here …

So

    Let me drink the BLACK water!

INSTRUCTIONS FOR YOUR NEW OSIRIS

Canopic old Egyptian jugs,
The jars in her boudoir hold me.
Or used to
Since she's moved them
Put them in her bag
And toted them to her new lover's house

That's what she throws in my face
Since she no longer holds me
Since she can't stand to stay around
No longer

My heart's in one

I'm dead
    because no longer does my body hold a heart

Another holds what's left of pride
The day my best friend laughed dead in my face
Because he knew she was his other best friend's
Lady

Another holds the essence
Of my self-respect
And still another, all my tenderness
For her

That's all.
    There's nothing left
But dead politeness

Not even passion left to kick her ass

She lies progressively to me
Each day, like the difficulty
Of game show questions
A little bitter more ridiculous each time
And unbelievable

Where is Gene Rayburn? Adrienne Barbeau?
George Gobel? Wally Cox? Familiar faces of the afternoon
Clifton Davis? Margaret Daniels?
It seems I just don't understand this show.

Lying, she cheats

In front my face, behind my back
It doesn't matter
The only novelty is tonight's choice
A movie with my girlfriend
Got a date, I really didn't think you'd be in town
Don't hate me do you? Please
Don't hate me please
I'm sorry, but I didn't think you'd mind
Of how she wants to let me know
We're through

When I was still alive, before I knew
The full name of the door,
I used to speak of her and say
"My Lady"

SHAKE HANDS WITH YOUR BETS, FRIEND

Every bookie
On the phone to Vegas
Odd
But all the trunk lines
Are tied up,
Sorry. This trunk is not seaworthy, sir.
In all good faith, I cannot
And other blasts from the past
No sir no good no sir
Such accents no longer seem strange;
Simply, they take their places
Next to the treasured linen in the trunk

Clean linen was prized so.

And silk, symbolic. Heraldry
Amid the horseshit; oriental mystery
Shining out imperial futures
Come a cropper in the knots of the dragon
Appliqued on the blouse
So carefully folded second down to the linen
And the silk tinted gold to go with the uniform serge
Of the master's desire for glory
Infecting all the crew with inertia
Obedience to the odds against survival
Cutting the Captain cutting
All of this loose, drifting free.

From the slaveship dock
Down dusty streets to auction block,
Awash in a chance for survival
No sir no good no sir
Until such accents no longer seem strange
He trudges

He drudges himself into choices before him
Using instincts and applied mathematical factors
The best advice is ask the winner
Bub, your guess as good as mine.

The choice is not acceptance nor adjustment
Nothing defiant definite at this time,
But give me a call in a day or two, he says;
From then on what? sack-cloth and cinders
Sandaled feet and a threatening sandwichman sign?

That's horseshit.
You either beat em or join em
Pays your money and you takes your choice
Everyone's a winner
EVERYONE'S A WINNER!
And other stale blasts from the past
No sir no good no sir
You'll be out there all by your lonesome!

Silks and silver fittings,
Your lonesome!

Riding free
To the roses, arched into the lucky horseshoe
A horticulturist piece against natural resistance
Circular winnings of really knowing the odds
Not even enjoying *A Day at the Races*
As it appears on late night TV yet again
At least the umpteenth time, but a respite
Of inexorable glee amid the usual horseshit
Resistance is natural, at first
Its lifeless monument
Suppression seems to rule
That's the usual horseshit

Show me a man

I sit here, for some reason, listing
Possibilities and ideas for packing a trunk
Or a kerchief
But leaving now is really going nowhere
New, not phrased or worried so bad
But confusing, that's what runs through
My mind concocting an elegant logic

Show me any slavery

A confusion of mail-order brides arrives
With careful trunks of hope and promises
Clutched in the letter packets in their hands
As dreams go sailing
Well damn how many *did* you send for sir
No sir no good no sir
You've got to choose

Off-track betting parlors are stormed!
Jostling
Throngs pushing and shoving
Thinking, soon he will choose.
Every bookie on
The phone to Vegas
People getting trampled down in the streets
In the mad rush to the window
As dated futures fling themselves
Into space from the top of office buildings
State capitols, from islands of pompous parkways
Skirting the miserable ghetto
They fling themselves on ignorant traffic
Short-tempered, sacrificial and vain
The drivers cuss the winged hopes on their heels,
Hoping to get home for supper
Before something else ruins their day
Knowing that when he chooses he will choose
As he has chosen
As have they themselves
Finally, to dare no more than one dares

To live so that one will not be forgotten
Buying that bit of immortal stroking
Piece by piece, by smile or favor
By appropriate chastisement or unnotice,
Not knowing though that though his choice is set,
This time when he places his bet
He's dealing with a new measure of chance.
But he doesn't know it may be the last time

III

The Marvelous Land of Indefinitions

You know, life is just a puzzle . . .
—Roosevelt Sykes

THE MARVELOUS LAND OF INDEFINITIONS

The poet's business is telling the truth.
—Ricardo Miro

How nice! How convenient!
We have all gathered to read & listen to poems
As if everyone were actually equal
Laborers in the corn fields
Girls in the cigarette factory
Though someone always seems to be saying
"A poet's task is making poetry . . . blah blah blah!"

But poeting with poor people doesn't end poverty.

How sweet it is! How nice!
First poems and last words
Are heard here, dedicated to friends
Describing the ultimate artistic inspirations
Incorporating all the latest stops and turns
Of fashion

Example the alleys oh like psychedelic birds
& the transfiguration of being,
of self, of the essence, blah blah blah
It's annoying.

Clearly, this poetry reading
Will not be heard in the town square
Because people don't listen to poetry
Since poetry is "the nectar of the gods"
And these readers are demigods
Raising up to nirvana and adulation
All of those others who read, write,
Or listen to this stuff
So
Tranquilly, everyone reads
After cocktails
embraces

Happily, an interesting poem
Reminds me of Proust
Or something from a 16th-century French book
Afterward
No one assumes responsibility for sense or vision
Because, in the final analysis, poetry
Is something personal
        intimate
        alien

Newspaper headlines are full of lies
And the radio is full of lies
AND POETRY IS FULL OF LIES!

Because everyone goes along
In slavish style follows the ways of the world
(European, Anglo-Saxon, White)

And the *style*, the *form* is what's important
Incomprehensible to everyone else
But them. Oh, in the final analysis
Everyone else is a part of the problem
And we're in the "in" crowd.

The ones who never read are ready to gossip!
Did you see so & so's new book?
        I just got accepted in *Reader's Digest*
Blah blah blah

But that's OK
        OK because we made the best of it
Seated at god the father's right hand
OK because here where nothing's happening
No one can truthfully say
                        us least of all
That we're lazy
Hate to work,
Know nothing but gambling, drinking, *fiesta*, good sex
(the common definition of a Panamanian)
                                        because

What's on our minds is the office
security, the kids.
Daily bread.
A payday every two weeks or the 30th

Everyone goes along
Because unemployment goes up every day
It's OK exploit the farm workers
OK that rent keeps going up
OK
that young people are lost in marijuana and "free love"
OK
because all the world drinks Coca-Cola and smokes Viceroys
And everyone prefers blonds and white folks
And cathedral arched eyebrows
OK
because the gringos don't worry themselves about anybody
(Only duck hunting in January—and that not too often—
And controlling the nation's economy)
OK
because it's the others who suffer

In the final analysis, this is the 51st state
In the wonderful land of indefinitions
Where everyone goes along
Where poets gather to read poems
And sip cocktails
And talk har har har
Chat har har har blah blah blah
Talk har har har
To evade the compromise
Escape the moment
Avoid facing destiny and the "secret word"
Each day growing clearer
Each day blah blah blah
Hovering blah blah blah
Nearer

(Roberto MacKay)

WHEN DUKARDO BOARDED THE ASTRO-JET, HE ALREADY DONE SEEN THE MOVIE

after Dukardo Hinestrosa

At an altitude of 9,000 feet
Above the simple level of my being
People seem all the same size
Whether Rockefeller or any child of Sanchez

Impossible to distinguish if they wear
Patent leather shoes or be completely naked.
If they have wisdom teeth still
Or gold fillings or go toothless

It's impossible to know if their faces
Are popular with beards or with lice
Or if the faces are regularly razored
With a Gillette, vehemently blue;

If they possess a lung of stainless steel
Or contact lenses. Or if the brain
Has been washed and dried in the sun
If their midriff has a plump Gordian knot
Or if the color of their toenails is enameled
Lazily red

If on their heads now has begun
The interrupting drop
Of southern showers
Or the strokes of an epileptic hammer
Judiciously answering
The basal metabolism of each one.

At 9,000 feet in a jet
When the motors by reaction form
Millions of revolutions per second
It's impossible to know with certainty
Who suffers, below, from complexes
And who is freudianly infirm

It's impossible I suppose to suppose
If their fingertips are as clear
As water. If their fingerprints have been traced.

If, in spite of everything, the salt
Of their tears may be iodine

Or if their sex is compromised
With new birth-control pills
Promising to create no more beings
Destined for a radioactive mushroom

From 9,000 feet in the air on an Astro-jet
It is natural:

Everything is very difficult to distinguish

HOME X XI

Just come back from the zodico
Alone
Call my long-distance girl friend
Her boyfriend answers,
"Yeah? Lorenzo who?"

I come back to this place
But this place ain't mine.

Just come back from the zodico

Alone
Where your girl friend
Her boyfriend says oh yeah and who is you
Yeah

I just come back someplace
But this someplace ain't mine.

MMDCCXIII ½

The cruelty of ages past affects us now
Whoever it was who lived here lived a mean life
Each door has locks designed for keys unknown

Our living room was once somebody's home
Our bedroom, someone's only room
Our kitchen had a hasp upon its door.

Door to a kitchen?

And our lives are hasped and boundaried
Because of ancient locks and madnesses
Of slumlord greed and desperate privacies

Which one is madness? Depends on who you are.
We find we cannot stay, the both of us, in the same room
Dance, like electrons, out of each other's way.

The cruelties of ages past affect us now

An excerpt from BIG HOUSE MOVIES

If any man were willing to change places, his ancestor would be a fool. In that one thought, the danger of the motion picture image reveals itself. Movie-watching is a Quixote's contest with the romance of non-being. It is an escape from the ego and the fears generated by the being of others.

Those others are the source of the ego's distractions, yet all of us are trained to rather not be ourselves. While fearing others. And what we fear in others is that they will interrupt the course of our own ambitions, or that they will support those ambitions and, in that way, hinder the accomplishment of our own disgust with ourselves.

Those sympathetically disposed to our success, especially that which has already been accomplished, might inspect their commitment before they are suspected of faint hearts.

Please pass the amyl nitrate.

One will appear quietly in the doorway, striped in the light from barred windows. A smile and a confessorial tone ensure no disassociation from decadent complicity in the world's varied violations of your threshold. The world is the others.

Every Big House movie has such a scene because that's what the TV set and the hugged-up drive-in folks want to see. The scene dramatizes what they believe to be the actual facts of their lives. A whispered word at the time-clock: "They're out to get you." A word from a wise guy is ordinarily sufficient to open the armory of paranoia's fleet mothball notions ...

Entire nations are being mothballed!

The doorway is the doorway to a closet
and your skeleton is inside, caught in a holdup

This scene is restricted, indeed, it is seldom actually shown on screen. It is the disturbing framework of the scenes that actually are screened. Ordinarily all of this is hidden in spoken narrative or dialogue of some sort, for we could not bear to watch it. No one wants to see the door closed, nor does anyone want the skeleton to break out (the Big House movies use the underworld argot "bust out") of its closet.

On another level, the entire rational spirit of nations mothballed in Christendom is viewed with fear and distrust. Yet all of that, too, is part of us. Which part is a game of "guesses, anybody" . . . just to keep the game going. But, for our own sakes, where the game is going should not be left up to guesswork.

Again, this is a dangerous psychological ledge . . . a case where "edge" is disadvantage. Say the secret word and then duck! After all, nobody likes a smart.

Samaritan! you cry to yourself. Suddenly, on the screen that monopolizes your sight, yourself multiplies into surly pickets. "Samaritan," you cry out in despair. And your other selves chant, "Pass 'm by!"

What are they all hepped up about? Something in the scenario that seems to escape you but, since you are paying attention, means something. And that something is threatening.

The problem of the mothballed nations. It touches the same psychological overload line. The very popular Zombie movies flirt with this reaction in the selves of the viewers. We are willing to put up with the antics of the walking dead because we are assured that they, in recompense for their post mortem mischief, will be reduced to dust at the end of the photograph. But in the case of *actual* entire mothballed nations we have no such assurance.

The Zombie and Big House movies represent only the tip of the iceberg. In their own way, the Jack Johnson and Iceberg movies touch on the nerve endings of the public psyche and batter us as if we were Titanics. We live our lives like ships that pass in the night.

Our stunted love blinks red and green, port and starboard, like an indecisive traffic light. Even our belated cries for help go out as redundant stutterings SOS SOS SOS like the redundancy of the motion picture frames fooling us into commiseration with the film's wraiths of light. And we love those phantoms of the Loew's, even as we fear human others. Andrea Dorias list in each one's imagination, in the oceans of their heads behind western eyes, a frighteningly real possible thing.

"Don't look now, but ..."

Or the childish game that ends in embarrassment. Well, if you knew your fly was zippered why did you look down! Huh?

—The others laugh and look down.

You think, *I'm a fool to fear.* But the steel guitar does not come in behind you. No drums. No fiddle. You were right in the first place ... the agony starts all over again as the next scene fades into sight.

This is exactly the effect of going to the movies or cheaply watching last year's flops on TV. The scenarios are each of them elaborate versions of that kid stuff. Open fly.

Big finale: The car pulls up to the door of the mansion just in time, rustling the leaves in the drive. That's in the Upper Class movies. In the Big House movies, there is no such saving chase. You and your ego are left in the doorway, fearing the close of the door ... striped in the theatrical light from barred windows ... annoyed by a preacher and a screw.

Scream your guts out. No one will hear you. If they do, they will lean over and say *Shhhhhhhh, I'm trying to hear.*

But this is old stuff. What filmed personal disaster accomplishes in testing the individual psyche (ego, you & me against the world), the Disaster films perform on a yet coarser scale. In the Disaster movies the dangerous others are dehumanized and, in that sense, made entertaining. Just like electric dishwashers.

Nancy Pickett says that in Cathay they had a habit of burying servants when the mandarins died. In the same burial mound. As times changed, good help became hard to get. So they started making porcelain servants.

Nowadays we have dishwashers and egos. The egos are merely spiritual leaks that need washers. But we also have needs and human fears, and good help is so hard to find. So God invented the movies. These eyeball enemas flush the brain of any sensible concern.

SCREEN TEST

Don't count the time lost, neither …
—Robert Browning

Consider thoughts to live
In life
In golden coils,
Her spirit clasps you
Hugs you close
To learning life's considerations
Gamely flutter
Pennants panties
Scenes badly-lit
In old movies
On the sheet tacked up
On the wall
Off the wall
Jazz solos against space
Feeling the people's sigh
Or soft voice harmonies
Describing the origin of sighs:

A volcanic garden.
Dark-panelled walls
Dusty dim Tiffany lamps
Pictures of Burn-out Johnson
Shutting em down
At Daytona or Supernationals
Scoring a long-disputed TKO over
Underrated Kid Flash

The quiet Paddock Bar in New Orleans
The Tack Room in Hot Springs
Beneath Bold Ruler's fading portrait
Our booth
Embraced in privacy's dim recall

The gentle homing instincts of a life
Spent well and gently
In a world's turmoil: The green of sporting felt
Color television astroturf
Pointilliste lawns & formal gardens
All silence yearning

To operate the mind in three dimensions,
Smoke if you've got em
Sleep lightly in American accents
Sighs

Bartered like any other eloquence
Remembered, quoted

Prizes of some moment, far or recent
Shining in memory
Hollywood premiere searchlights
Scanning neon-blushing skies
For stars more brilliant
Than those whose limos birth them on the pavement
Impressed by the footprints of other earlier average
Americans who ascended in biograph light

Lips pout
Or catch the tongue between their fulsomeness
To seize her sighs
And still his questionings
Teeth flash and click,
Recover earlier imposter accents

A line vanishes
smudge
The words flee into telephonic moments
The silent poses that accompany the voice
Across charged ethers grown heavy with manners
And distance's natural doubts

Echoes of our accents fortify us
Against these moments when the posse betrays
Us only to ourselves
The foot put right the proper laugh
Imposter phone booth shush a pirate haven

All our theatrics spring from private laws
Losses and moments, the first time seeing ourselves

Wrongly, a line vanishes
In a split second's prodigalness
Receiver cocked to the wrong ear
An inappropriate surmise of levity
His awkward charm
The others' puzzling elaborations

First, the pose. Then the posse

A self-portrait would have it oh him

Though others shall continue their puzzles of faith
Faithless wit, agonizing self-eradications
Awkward charm and flea market momentous worries
"Ladybug, ladybug . . ." Such things happen.

Occurrences fill the morning radio like kisses
Or the working man's stale-mouthed recriminations
For example,
There's the show in the phone booth
The numbers quickly scratched on the wall
Desperate labanotations
An awkward pas forging ahead despite of
Interruptions

In woodlands, forests, open spaces
Now
We primp ourselves on country odors
Denim cigarette smoke breath of beer
Lite

Sunlit dust and shadowed forest streaming
Through the weft of garments and hair
And sunlit dust of pose around the phone
Speaking to distances in person

And, naturally, the distant ones in person
Have to be doing just the same to reconcile us
To the terror of our personal space. Space
Filling with all the dreams we decipher from logic
And late conversation

Recollection of the pose in the booth
Teddy Nadler, Eichmann, lover at the headache plateau
Reflection of the dance in the gloss of the glass
Facing the speaker with angles of traffic
And the breeze blowing through the smashed pane

This space missing the pane we take for granted
Taking this light show of our concern's affection
Granted, it's a moment's escape. A spectacle
Of awe for one's own attachments

Unwilling grace

Stubborn blessings dog the beaten heart
Like obnoxious but useful reporters
Tripping over microphone cords,
Stumbling in Charles Laughton's profound footprints
Retiring into the light

All of the all of the all of the feeling, bold
Reduced to a mismanageable ease
A cartoon. 20th Century Fox logo footage
Universal's glass world,
Daring Wiley Post aeroplane
Circling a world premature record
Amelia Earhart disappearing curtsy women's lip
Introducing performance
Of disguised boredom and banality

Blaaaah! And classic violin concerto
Classic horrors (plucked from grave,
Collaged from charnel house, the living
Dead)

Footprints handprints dentured kisses in the stone
Ghoulish commonplaces of celebrity
Glees manufactured not to be forgotten

& other commonplaces:
Dancing dots
Kyle's Egyptian block in Beaumont, Texas
Modern art nouveau

Yes, why does popular America persist in death dreams?
Kyle's in Beaumont. Modern times, King Tut?

Paramount's cartoon McKinley soaring
Bound with stars
Above the motion picture beneath it
"All they show these days," says Duke, "is garbage"
Purposeful poses of the seeking lost
Childish posses
Kindly portraits of urbane Josephites
Columbia's animated Aphrodite
Luciferous gem of the ocean
Twinkling in comic-strip butterfly light
Stolen from dreams to illumine
Dull turns of mannered script

The cursive swirl and curl of RKO Radio music
Different so in these days of motivation
As if sounds were not memories also,
As if motivations are not remembered old tunes
"The story unfolds ..." Pictures of pictures in disciplined tone range
Xerox
Black & white

Consider, girl, these images to live
In life
In golden coils,
In thoughts recovered
Hip postures of faded stagings
4,000 whisperings in darkened halls,
"*King Lear*, Act 1, sc. iii"
To stay the guilt of trashy tabloids
Wrinkled ephemerides
Which feature every star's comings
And goings on

Can I mention "Round Midnight" here
As she reads me the Bible? I will
Probably consent in the morning, seeking a word
The word one word to remember
And the posings just shuffle along
Congregations, medleys of ancient hit tunes
Into and out of your mind
Consider life itself to be a puzzle
Like a highway as it appears on a map

Consider you yourself lost in a delta
Of a sudden river you did not expect
Did not expect this woman did not anticipate
The toilsome burdens of a simple space
Touching her hand, romantically feeling shy
When shy you've never been in all remembrance

Be careful how you touch her
She may awaken …
Within her dreams it seems to him he's something special
Oh him
Before she awakens to make up her mind,
Before she hides her face in her dream,

A fear exists that's packaged in illusion
Like seeds in their packets
Like verses of a song heard somewhere

Considered in a particular pastime moment
With her or without her
All of it coming clearly to mind

Her life and his exemplified in golden coils
Cardioid warmth, images and music
Attending pose each pose and change of mind
Your fascination stepped-up and refined
Modulated by the flickering changes of light
As the movie goes from the drawing room
To the chaise everyone's been talking about
Soft, loving light in the close-up
The first time you kiss her. The chase ends.
The movie ends. Headlights go on like candles
As the tornado looms in the screen door

Her head on his shoulder, sleeping prettily
Softly, as he drives home
Singing catches of the hits on the radio
Lost in the Beatles, seeing her pretty
Strayed and exiled in the changes of some insinuating blues
Seeing the headlights pass in curls around her hair
Studied in affection's sidelong glances
Now & then. At any other time, hands on the wheel!
Eyes firmly on the road!

Like our poor memories of Hot Springs afternoons,
The loving conversations as other bettors wailed,
The blues pulse out their crude approximations
Somber, in kinks of words we barely hear to understand
We only recognize familiar turns of music

She'd cry if she was wakened
Or is it you the only one who'd weep
For her awakening
Tears for your own déshabillage of esteem's emotions
And guilt to woo the weeping

The lie confirms
The strongest instinct is to beg the question
Oh him and beg it further
My luck damn sure is looking up
These days, it smiles and cares
In nearness now beside me, in my hand
Even the distance wishes fortune & a smile

Illusion stops
Stock still
It stopped stuck
Like a TV football game in instant replay
A mighty wave of joy
A zzzing radio zzzzzzz
Pretty cheerleader in a cowboy hat
Arched in a japanese woodblock
Hiroshige moment
Stolen frozen Chosen

And oh! if she awakened
Oh what sorrow!

To see too much in a moment of him
Overseen like First National's lot
Acres of quonset huts and block buildings
Where passably creative magic churns
To fill dull weekends at the country drive-ins
With schemes and joy and terrors of teen hearts
Vaguely intent on these plottings

Hung here in space extravagant wallpaper
Willingly mutable to squeeze a smile,
A happy reminiscence, sense of portent,
Laughter, homely yearning, adrenal rushes

Oh him (this time a mystery movie), *some* delicious response
From those who are preoccupied with yearning!

Kaleidoscopic tear?

Consider, then, in life,
In golden coils of daily expectation
The certain fear persists
That she may wake and weep
That slightly parted sleeping lips
Will speak and name you clearly

Joyful nods and elbow prods of recognition
Sweep your fandom.

God

You can either sit facing the jukebox
Standing in interminable popcorn lines
Missing the credits
Facing the future soundless on the other screen
A tabloid smile for the birdie
The photograph that will eventually appear
"In Happier Days" if you want to,

You can appeal to a guarded fanatic within you
Bleating "amen" in a pleasure, like a child's
Indefinable and beyond transcription
Except a buoyant quality of warmth
In a climate growing dark with indecision
Where skies are white as envelopes
And the Liberty Bell on the stamp floats like an airship
Bearing dreams, snapshots, and loneliness complaints

Tears and heats of absence grows this fear
The harvest clutters every drawer and cranny
With glimpsed impediments
Half-served considerations
Faces and hours curled on the cutting room floor,
To be nostalgic and romantic about it—
Priceless bebop 78s she scratched beyond repair
Giggling. Or clumsily sat on.

Or you can go create yourself
Great power and joy in your exiles
Contemplating "Three Years of Torture"
Percy Mayfield's murky bayou of a voice
Spilling into all around and through the house
Through perennial cardboard cones
Reminding you of pinetrees and magnolias

Smiling, waving as the flashbulbs awaken
Adroitly graceful, gliding around Alan Ladd's
And Mickey Rooney's elevator shoeprints
Barely, acknowledging the screaming throng's flirtations
Secure in the coils of her love and her distance,
Her head resting on your shoulder. And you, poised,
On the threshold of cleverer interpretations.

CLASS ACTION

One person amplified one hundred
Thousand times
Assumes that he
Or she must be, at least, wallpaper
As important as that

(At least) as being on the radio calling the jock
Dedicating on the air one temporary tune
Composed by amateurs and marketed by pros
To Junior and Susie, Diana with her fine self
JT and Bobo, P.P. and Poppa, Willie Rae,
That tired old Delois
                                        watch yourself now brother man
Hey
            sweet sweet Sally,
From the little bitty one to Mister Heartbreaker
Two Ten-Four and Wild Turkey
They know who they are
                                        heh heh
The "Astoria Queens"
                                        Yeah

Who do you   wa   tch   tch now, watch it!
            think
Who do you think would send this out to you
                                                                                Yeah
LT from South Park
                                        check it out, baby
Sending it all out
                                        for you
Sending it
            all   sending this one out for the Sunnyside children
Beautiful Lady Jo, with her bad self
                                                            oh yeah

Margaret Anne, Rapunzel & all the guys
down
To the Possessive Tower Physical Fitness Center
yeah
All
Who have chosen this particular hit to justify our time
Spent dancing to it, and clarify the meaning of our times

A
Three or four hundred years
Go whistling by
The graveyards of perception
Like in a 1930s movie,
Self-serving histories of the self-serving
What really killed Vaudeville

Calendars flipping crazily, newspaper headlines
Twirling into the sidewalk's sudden view,
The blind man in the kiosk groping toward the NEWS
Was the wallpaper, shrunk-sided
Art Deco filling the movie houses of the plains
Venetian palaces in potato-land
Putting all the blacks in the loft
Keeping them in segregated places
Above the ushers stationed by the stairs
To herd them ever upward

That the orchestra escape infection of the Blues
Red-suited ushers guided us aloft
While white Americans below were entertained
By wraiths of aberration on the screen
All black & white to them, all hats and horses;
To us, variations of blues, as the light rose
And churned in the vault of the house and cigar smoke
Swirling toward our ordained roost

Balcony wallflower seats
Formerly reserved for the nobles
In the days they were still sane
In Europe

We spat on the groundlings from there
From our balcony quarters
Which made Genet call us niggers
Jujubes rained down to the floor
Matting the cornsilk heads of Doom's scions

We chewed the Jujubes before we hurled them

In Africa, the spirits pout
For stardom on the silver screen

Silver has blue in it, plus black and white
And passes for one thing and another
if you spend it right

We are the wallpaper fraying
Out of woodwork anchors
We are asking questions and question answers
Too vague to be forgotten for their haste

There is really nothing to get all upset about

Nothing chronic answers a child's curses

Nobody gives a damn what niggers say
Calypso songs are spoofed & pooh-poohed every day.
In Africa, the spirits pout;
The militants think they'll win
Without a doubt, there is something going on
But really nothing to get hot about

Proverbs are lozenges in dusty peach
Prophecies swirl in borders near the floor

We are the wallpaper.

Scrolling outward, withered in the heat of answers
Formed in hate and haste
And all the waste of time on aberration
Considered "entertainment" in our time

While spirits pout, we others spot and fade
Spinning with fortune like unspooling film
Unleashing great comedians and pissed-off heroes,
Doomed ingénues expiring without perspiring
In molten gardens filled with sighs and silent
Movie glances

That's entertainment
                                        the force of circumstance
Is stronger than one thinks
It draws on everything and riddles hope
Circles the future on our calendars
Claims all the past its own
                                        as memory's "I told you so"
As indiscriminate as vacuums clutching air

Each vision (even simple sight, foresight,
I told you so) is what is sheltered from this force
Which wouldn't necessarily harm it
The way air unthinkingly crushes its absence
To entertain the kids in Physics I
Circumstance would rather surround it
An invisible shield
A force field of a 1930s fantasy.
Vision would shrink from lack of danger
A tunnel of hot security and boredom
A searing light cylinder of lens projection
Saved from the clumsiness of needed dreamers

That's life
              motion pictures you've seen and forgotten
The plot or the message
                          even the stars

Only continuity remains
Attention that abides within each moment
Filed in recollection
Opens in repose, touching the flesh
With actual motion

Fingertips glow slightly, lips and eyes
Juggle flickering smiles and heavy sighs

Like wallpaper, America designs
Ourselves
Projections in the dark
Children of genius whose inventions
Include the ferris wheel,
Passing the buck,
The choking sky, a genealogy
Stolen to wanting mothers
Who disguise each fear as love, each want as discipline
Sometimes in anger
Bright with this heritage, we push
Our minds father logical jazz

What shall I do but speak
In Africa, the juju spirits shout through us
Our screams speak rapture of their presence,
Not our pain (which is unutterable).
Without them, we would live in silent movies
Which now bereft of Orpheums or Hippodromes,
Apollos or Bijous, would have us acting out our lives
In Five Oaks 6s, Midtown Twins,
And anagrams of corporate collusion

In Africa, the spirits gad about like niggers
Long, shiny shone shoes! Amazing limousines
With music blasting speeding to heaven and back
On superhighways carved from inspired trees!
And that ain't nothing

If I should speak, the wallpaper would break
Its silence, too.
Should I despite some fiction of myself
To talk, as the wallpaper should?
Should I forget myself because spirits are talking
Or pleas to you or yourself or your master
When, obviously, no plea does no good

And any plea at all does little better
Than simply being there, like the woodwork;
Working yourself up like wallpaper.

Hurling Jujubes down on their heads,
The ones who fear the Blues unless they're silvered,
In the darkened theater
Does as little good as the pleasure of being ignored
Being stolen away from yourself
One casual phrase at a time, or suddenly
A traumatic abduction from your own projection
Anxious yes and easeful as your "own"
Or after slackening of care by days
Being looked at as if you were wallpaper;
As strategy, it isn't logical a bit
But if it works, it's a breakthrough to logic.

Unlettered negroes called this logic Jazz
Relating thought to life, love to projection
Spirit entertained by spirit
as in life
And when the movies chose to speak
the voice was Jazz
Projected through the fantasy of aberration
For which the blame accrues to those who thought
That anyone was free to choose among spirits
Like segregating folks
or seating suckers at the picture show.
The logic holds its own
configuration

Patterns of light of thought of sound must move
Patterns are meant to bounce away
From walls; the ones that stick there . . .
Kente cloth moves when woman works
to praise the weaver
While flattery and hate speak without guile
to the believer
A hunter sharpening his knife

Is honing eyes   to flesh the spirit
From the tree into his life; and
The musician, cranking keys and twining strings
Imagines he can hold his voice inside his hand

These things are true, told beautifully
They sometimes teach us to sleep, to learn there
That truth is beautiful while we are sleeping.
We are entertained by turns of logic
Flickering upon us with a grain of sense
Strained carefully from daylight, like a dream.
But rudely told, the truth just spreads.
Discretion lost, it multiplies its faces
Shimmering
Like a voice understood pealing outward
Ringing and extending its reach
Preening its facets to make echoes jealous

If no one speaks, the truth will still
Be true. Poor thing, unspoken.
False friends snickering behind
Her back, echoes piping up
With snide conceits
All about English lakes and valleys wild
Paul Whiteman's greatness & all that jazz

In Africa, the spirits kiss their teeth

Wallpaper oh?

The second power of arithmetic is grammar
Disguised as laws, as favors, getting over
Getting it together, getting straight
Just for a minute getting straight for what it feels like
Keeps you poor. That's what it feels like.
Feeling poorly
For just a minute, put a sad smile on your face
The badge of honored membership in the inhuman race
Toward contortions of emotion known as Art

When other people spend the money. Considered
Guile and in cahoots when you're important.

Ain't it the truth?

You're blessed.
You don't have to decide which which is which
Just got to feel it
Don't have to give a damn
If you don't care,
Someone will explain what you would say
If there was anything you could say
After all your vast experiences against the wall

Fading there, drawn on
ripped-off
Finally, if you won't speak
dream
That student radicals will
Provide a new generation of protest
Crazy posters upon your foundation
That happy families or anarchist avant-gardes
Will superimpose their slides and films
On your strong patterns
A waste of space
Disguised as privacy, as thoughts, as getting even
Show them all
yeah

You've got strong backing
yeah
But it's up against
the wall

You're getting flakey.

Behold the spirits,
With their lips poked out,
They look just like the people in the street

Who wind in patterns of elated doubt
And depressing certainties
That send them jogging circles around life
Just like the movie people reel around
Sane conversations in real restaurants
And their own private swimming pools,
Trapped in the truthless patterns of the light
That entertains us in the darkness of our lives
Where papered walls compete with littered streets
For eloquence

We succumb to all mythologies of moments
All so subtly disguised as loss of care
Liquids that turn to film and film to powder
Tripping, getting off
Up till our lives are filled with minuses
Or finally we cling to one alone,
Everything is true but us about us.

And I'm a lie! Because I see in twos or threes,
Because my view is amplified by night
Crazily flies into the dawning sun
Cussing & fussing like it supposed to bes
A natural man
Because my spirit slaps me upside my head
And makes me turn to see the others pouting
Because by lack of eloquence
I'm left here to embarrass you by shouting
That we must speak or be like patterns on a wall,
Moving or pasted still, it doesn't matter much

            You don't have to take my word
For "it"

HAT RED

The earth remains the kind of saucer Sally saw in the decadent gardens of the upper East side on the night of the day of the great blackout.

Remember the silly Rosh Hashanah on the 17th floor? The sillier Yom Kippur in Evanston noticing for the first time the horns on the roof of the Illinois Central station? That's why Monk has got to wear that silly pork pie hat.

The UFOs hung calmly in the velvet pitch above the dimmed skyline, their radios monitoring unintelligible broadcasts of Lyndon Johnson's unintelligible Texas drawl. Lyndon was wringing his hands. Lindsay was wringing Mike Quill's bull neck *in absentia*. Somehow the TWU was behind it, he knew it. But somehow they were not the culprits this time.

Dim-lit cabarets got mucho dimmer. The combos played the sinking liner songs. "Good-bye Dodge Boy Hat" segue "Be it ever so humble—there's no place like home." "Clark in the Dark." All by ear. Damn sure couldn't read no music. Huh!

From the rim of the saucer, the terrain dipped gracefully toward a silken palisade across the Hudson. It could be seen as a darker, shiny black against the black. And somewhere eons away a burn-off stack at an Esso plant in Camden flickered in the blackness like a red feather in a Harlem cowboy hat. 50s version. A smooth curving blackness was the earth's jealousy of the sky's vault that poets and artists had been prating about since the days of Michael Angelo, one of their capos.

Beep buboop! Beep beep bubop! You know how they invented all those words.

I know this is all true because I woke up on the F train at the last stop 179th St after falling asleep on my way home from work, the hard work and the downers did that. And when I woke up, all the lights were off and the train was deserted and I remembered Baraka's *Dutchman* and got scared and thought O shit can this be some kind of a joke or is this the end or is this the end of the line or the last stop again or the world hunh. Some of these questions went through my ha ha mind. And in the street on top of the station confusion was literally raining or reigning. The only lights were the headlights. And my head had gone out! The busses were full of smirking people the bastards while the subway riders did Chicken Little bits on the sidewalk. Their heads had done gone out.

My feet lightly touched on the ground.

Two young girls down 169th St bearing candles giggling saying "Pilgrim, blessings upon thee" as I ran into Triboro Records to see if the music was going if Ric thought this trip could be real. Ric said, Hey man, can you dig this? So I figured something had to be usual, even if I was still in the dark. What the hell.

Who is this fool in the comic cosmic zootsuit gaucho slouch brim hat? The only light the glistening pearl in his hat band. And shouldn't there be a light in the window?

At home, the folks were listening to emergency WNEW radio dumb show broadcasts kerosene generator-style just like way off back in the country or Nha Be, Viet-Nam detailing how Lyndon was in Washington DC the comparatively City of Light at the moment, wringing his hands. Wondering how he could get the Air Force into JFK Int'l Airport to keep orders lessen the Viet Kongs snuk in under covers of darkness (just they style) and do some strange number while the streetlights was dozing and the nigger catchers (strontium light) slept in the UFO darkness of a sudden technological Cimmeria at the edge of the earth. But goddammit in New York City?

Hush your mouf! That's Nixon style. Get back, Baudelaire! It was getting to getting that deep. The peoples was frantic and suddenly very uncool. De dark ages.

Sun Ra considered the whole thing amusing. For several weeks after all the lights went on again, he smiled as if to say I told you so and kept showing us a clipping from the *National Enquirer* that reported to show flying saucers hovering all over the city. It was to die! Skeptics insisted it was no flying saucers but glare on the photographer's lens. Glare from where?

We sure felt dumb. Sitting there in the dark looking stupidly into the glistening of each other's eyes. That is, if you were smart enough to have a candle.

"Don't just stand there looking like a wet dream, do something!" And "what the hell you want *me* to do! Do I look like goddam Con Ed to you?" Brother against brother. And so on. Although, even in the light of all that, the light stayed Off.

And it wasn't until the next several hours, after the devil smiled and tipped his Hatlo hat, and the shine from the bald head underneath the black crown turned up the sunlight like an Ace in a tight moment at the table when all your goddamm money's all most gone, you know. Yes, it was just the smile of the other side of the hat.

The heat was off. And inside the enigma was shiny silk lining turning silly silk nuance colors in the light and gold well "gold" anyway initials monogrammed on the sweatband. A distinct change. And thank goodness gracious. The hat, in the sudden natural daylight, was shaped like a cardinal's hat (the black one they wear in the daytime, not the red one for the holy parade). Nevertheless. Sometimes even now all these years later, off downs and sober except for the six-pack of Falstaff, I shudder to think.

What if he'd been wearing the red hat, the one with the cute little tucks and points on the sides . . . the cardinal points . . . how would *that* have gone down?

Gentile Horus!

It's a lucky thing we're so lucky. It's like we have to keep on making errors and having the cosmos surprise us. But we always seem to be able to lick it. Even if it means stick sticking it out (whatever the sticky situation) till the sunrise. Or any old other natural same old Egyptian so-called Roman thing.

Owhhh!

I'm so breathless because this is too true. And it's still true today. It did happen for true and I saw it. Or did not see it, that is, I mean in the darkness. And there is a many true words in this story of that day there *was* a night in New York City. Some of the holy ones are articles and verbs nouns and so forth. It was a sign from greater powers than we be and, so sadly, few of we on earth have heed the signals hidden there and then in that dark.

I don't know about no UFO, but I do know Anne weeps for all sentient beings. And I know my brother Ishmael cusses. I'm too mean for either of that. But I tell you, it's a goddamn lucky thing we're so lucky.

CLEAR CHANNEL

Ha ha. You searching
For money
Find affection.
An object found

Touched by that one's hand

Kirlian fetish

This is supposed to go on
Without interruption
Until something surprising
Emerges or surfaces and

Contemplates the reversal:

For an instant
Teardrops and raindrops
Ascend like fountains,

Then back to gravity clichés

It's all your fault, Edgerton!

IV

Liquid City

You better not gamble . . .
—Huddie Ledbetter

Break a vase, and the love that reassembles the fragments is stronger than that love which took its symmetry for granted when it was whole.
—Derek Walcott

SALT

after Ovidio Martins

I was born a speck of sand
Thus I engulf the oceans
All the oceans in the world

My couriers are waves
Who fetch and tote
My messages and secrets

My missives and epistles
Little nostalgic notes
Are highpriced briny sighs
Collected by the sirens
At the cresting of the tides.

Within the swirls and jeweled shells
Of all the oceans in the world
Dwell echoing confirmations
Of my love songs. I was born

A speck of sand
So I engulf the oceans

All the oceans in the world

DISCOVERING AMERICA AGAIN

In memory of Tom Dent

The world we found was not something
To fall in love with
But there were people in it
Who watched us at our games

Who warned us early
African veneers and European valences
Could both be false and
Polished surfaces distracting

Armed us with corny maxims
Pride is not assumed but earned
By effort properly applied

Common sense:
Garvey, Washington, Du Bois were men
Like those you meet in the street

And sent us on the way, expecting us
To be explorers
Space travelers in song,
Screaming or mellow
In caravans of ageless aspiration
To memorize exuberant manifests
Of semi-precious words

Discovering America again,
We found
The simplest of all mysteries
Called speech
Retains the register
Of fear
Encountering
What we do not know we know
Disguised as other people.

They are still there, those watchers
Watching you
Discovering America again

Don't be afraid—

Someone has walked this way before
All the world's music in her hands
Under the starlight
That she wished
Could lead away to freedom
Or at least a space to be
As newborn as tomorrow,
Forgiven as today

Someone has walked this way before
Who learned the secret

Someone has walked this way before:
A man who knew
That speech
Is breath made lovely
Shaped and shaping
Volume expanding both
Inside and out
In the quick transfer
Of sight and feeling
Into sound
                    and sense (sometimes)

Someone has walked this way before,
My friend
Who was my friend

A man who spoke with people
Who asked you questions
So that you could breathe

HAPPY NEW YEAR

after Tran Te Xuong (1870–1907)

Mother's as decked out
As a corpse laid out in rags

Uncle has a bandana as big as an awning
Old Auntie's skirt hem
Sweeps the verandah stair.

Virtue surely to walk in Buddha's steps
But a monk *must* have a parasol

Walking as if on air to his seat
In the railway coach

No.

No no . . . we are not wealthy
On this day of Tet

We are as down & out
As the owl, as those who wine
is green tea

SUMMER STOCK

after Tran Te Xuong (1870–1907)

Oho! It's the traveling opera!

We shout and scream and
actually weep

Even though the young Prince
is a bad actor

And the Emperor
In smeared whiteface
Is really so sad.

ART FOR NOTHING

The new dean asked
Where all my work
Had taken me
At the third stop, he said
“That’s my hometown”

Disguised behind my smile of pleasant interest,
The Medici in me rolled up his sleeves

You only get one chance
To make a first impression

“I loved it there! There’s so much happening
Folks are so friendly
The kids impressed me.   Really on the ball
Yep, great potential there
That’s a town that really has it all . . .”

“The week we moved there,” he said
“They lynched a man
Hanged on a big live oak
In the Court House square
All through the holidays
They let the body hang there

Said, This is our civic Nigger Christmas decorations
And set a watch so as we couldn’t cut him down”

Together, we both said
“Yep, that’s some town”

THINGS COULD BE WORSE

for Susan Joy in the Ozarks

I who have never given to you
But taken with every favor
I, who have sneered at meekness,
Pledge and vow
And every tender tentative gesture of care
Wrapping me closer to you
Though a hand's touch is as far away
As the patio light that shines on a leaf
Of prized caladium
Waiting for the dew that would glisten
That it might heat the dew into more subtlety

Life should be a gas!
Amazing buttes and roadside joints
Slide by unnoticed
Glum at the wheel of our cramped Winnebago
Fleeing into the cramp of the country,
I am jealous of the more contented in their cars
Mexicans Negroes & our own strayed breed
Old beat-up Valiants, radios loud
Over-priced vans full of stoned ne'er-do-wells
Transporting trust fund surfboards
Through the desert of our flight

You, without the children, brew up cares
Spoiling the view and demanding
Escape the confinement of space
That my impatience has made miserable,

Must admit that your closeness is precious
So precious
Absence makes me feel like someone grown
Well-liked and respected in a one-horse town
Airstream
For fleeing all celebrity and blame

Having been once a wealthy entertainer
Beloved franchisee or discount County judge
Leo Romero
In a late night television dream,
Brought back to fame in a special limited offer
Caught so drowsy in America's sleep
Singing nonsense songs to lonely losers
Who hear their own guilts laboring on the spools
Of temporary popularity
Made dearer by elapsing moments
Lapses gulp of fortune noted by the press
Of actual feelings creeping into mind

Loved, then, for settling
As an old house is not so ramshackled remembered
Headaches of not having the rent
Are easily construed to fits of fondness
Engorged with warming reliefs of surviving
First one's memories and, later, time
After time has distilled the harsh actual

At the entrance hall to the solarium:
The Corning ware anniversary blown up
In colored plexiglass based on the Polaroid pictures
Flawed Polavision nudist antics Airstream gleaming
Me and the kids behind you, smugly gleaming
The carport ceiling depicts in bronzed aluminum
Posting the banns, your sister's husband
Reeling drunk into the downstairs bathroom
A trail of cigar ashes on the brand new carpet
Me on the lawn with the birthday Weed Eater

It will be enough for me to accept this new fame,
Pleased with the secret of my scrapbooks
15 years being quietly weird without note
Knowing the genesis of my mildness
Only you
Recycled of the ragged consciousness of loneliness
Blurred nights and days becoming faint as footsteps leaving

While the kiss cools on the cheek
And arms ache from the last embrace
That common sense told us to break
To satisfy the artificial needs of all creatures:
Turtles.

The sparrow waiting at the hedge to be startled.
Children impatient to wave "bye"   A neighbor pleased.
This is the only lesson age has taught me:
If fear of nature or just mankind's tinkerings
Turtle's neck works

The magics of our youth return in our dual solitudes
To haunt us
Throat of a Christmas sweater knit with love
Though distant, delivered by United Parcel Service
Too large too small
Wool
Spinning and Sennett
Husbandry and coy devices
Flannel pajamas grown as we have grown
Stalking us all the days of our lives
Rotating and flapping
In amusements of clotheslines and dryers
Finally, now, catching up.   And,   again,   us.

Oh
Soft soft hair finally allowed to gray by nature
Outweighs any inflation of our golden years,
old woman

I didn't
Really
Need another pack of Luckies
Then
I need one now

Times like these, those
Are the things I remember.

The service in this restaurant is poor
And the girl from the office, while attractive
She's also young and greedy. She's a bore!

Aha
A *déjà vu* before your change
And my retiring

It's a good thing there's no current
In these circuits, you'd be shocked
Just to know the thoughts I've thrown away
Could help or harm you only if you knew
Betty Furness beside her Frigidaire
The duty of effort required to return
At last, without rancor or fear, simply and
Humbly to the blunt unvarnished statement

I who have given nothing cheer
Fully or under pain
Of facing what is true about evasions
Recognizing finally shortcomings
Are always built-in aspects of confession
I, who am taken with your unsure presence,
Have abandoned all hope of séance or phone call
Given up the dream of suddenly
Suddenly seeing you in that chair
Again

Admitting the cruelty of choosing not to please you
For fear that you would know that I'm pleased
I walked away for that, you know
To see or hear or touch you, near or far from me
Whatever elusive force connects us is persistent

It takes a man to say that

THE GODS' OWN PRIVILEGE

Oh, don't you hear me crying ...
—Chester Burnett

Orion boldly strides the southern sky
And walks the darkened sea

Lydia,
A troubled year
To learn the spider's art
Hidden in peril,
Safe in perdition's tangles
A boasting penitence

It is less punishment
Than polishing;
There are worse tortures
Than minute memories
Brightly vanishing into a golden dusk
Tie-dyed and swirling to the Grateful Dead

I sit, pencil in hand
Tangled in 30 feet of tape
Respooling the cassette
Twirling and straightening
Rewinding songs I already know

Shadows of lavalites
Syncopated dance of golden palms
Methedrine gospel breakdown
Echoes of Lydian song

Would there be thunderbolts,
Would there be lightning
The long slow freight with its careening lamp,
A ponderous rumble following
Pathway of the spark, going on
Three four hundred miles

Remembering thin nights in Colorado
The night we lay on the banks of the Same
River, afraid to go in
Would there be lightning
Would the next step take us
Vanishing
Into the pearl gray sky

The would be thunder weights each
Corner of the sky

Lydia,
I learned to touch you
Soft as you touched her
As you touched me

Lydia,
Like a slip of light
At the edge of an opening door
Trying to keep the quietness in

Inside the day that folds over night
Holding tightly
A scarf of starlight
Moving towards the cool
Of the spectrum

Dazzling motels on old postcards,
Red light begins to harden
Waiting to shatter like a vase
Priceless only in memory
Gone rigid in a clumsy kitten's path

Lydia,
How you touch me
Without touching
It's the light from each of us
Blending
Heat

Lydia
Softens

And so the string of lights,
Invisible, but imagined unbroken
Between the pointed appearances
Of Lydia
Brilliant gold hieroglyphs
Around your waist
Glimmering and bright
Then twirl into the darkness again
Or the flat untroubled foil of afternoon

Lydia,
Your strobe-like attention
Giggling beams and vanishings
Like money that outshine the moon

As
Is
A muted man disguised
In curbstone wisdom
Treasured vestiges of light
And foreign lifetimes
The light that merely waits
And reappears
The spark of knowing what it looks like already
So the photograph does not disappoint you

Lydia,
The light that merely waits
Was not guardian or guide
Isis aspin inside the zodico
If there are worlds to travel
And the words collect

SOUVENIR OF THE MANASSAH BALL

In truth,
Cordelia was a scorpion in blue
She called her divorce
"Independence Day"
You could hear the bombs bursting in air
She marched out like a majorette
And kicked her heels and cut her hair

"Pantomime Quiz" became the rage
At every party.
We danced around each slight and frown
A thousand brazen pairs of us
Rang in the city's chandeliers

We stung her way out of society
Then out of town

We found a charming cottage
In a nice suburb of Hell
Our tryst brought misspelled death threats
To her door:
A Barbie doll hung in a shoelace noose
A 10p nail driven between its legs.

But passion shields its servants from all harm
And her ex's wages kept the cottage warm

So, having stole the bride
Too late I knew
A misdirected Lochinvar
It's hard to assign victimhood
Or know who conquered who
She tied my ties
                    and combed my hair

I cooked for her
                    and read her books

Sometimes I was her splendid toy,
Sometimes her sword

And every moment thrilled our flesh with madness!

LIQUID CITY

I

This morning wakes
Sun all around my head
A small confused attempt with memory
All urge to pry
Out
Dusty leaves and shelves a song
On Nottoc mart tram cotton no
Song
Not grand relic remains in Houston
Of a derelict glory
La Carafe, sure
Glatzmaier's lunch Old
Market Square blazing in sun
A dream of builders

Hush
As Juke Boy sang
It's going to be a long long lonesome ride back home
It's going to be a long, long
Lonesome ride back home
As Juke Boy sang, something seemed wrong
Ain't nobody even missed me
All the time since I been gone

No song

A little sun,
White as a cotton bloom,
Rounded a boll or blossom
To blue dawn
Ripens to gold, and all blues
Green to noon
By fires by night, by clouds by day
No song

No song

Bring us, O givers
From towers stilted in this ancient bayou
Merchants and manufacturers
Bring us
Of survey transits, of plumbs
The tools &c intense volcanic sight
Sublime of mud commodity &c
Mud.

Up from the waters, a lush green
From the bayou from the landing
The urban the lush geology lapidary layers peel
First banks   then markets   horizontal
Shops   hotels   then Banks
In constant replicate year by year

With dreams of songs just waking
Piano player tinkle plunk tinkle Louisiana sound
Come 5th Ward, Texas
Silver Moon Café busy streets downtown
It's raining in the barren parks
The city first a dream of New Yorkers
By Abe & Pappy's
A city marching proud away
Shining from its countenance
Shining

No song

II

> *And yet I cannot find my own face.*
> *—James Wright*

No song
Sounds like eavesdropping at a cocktail party

Chit chat from strangers
About someone you'd rather not know

Facades of shining surface, blinding glass
More than a pile of stone and steel
Walls of mirrors stilted underneath
Rising above the green twine of the bayous

All brokedown W Dallas porch
A freedman named Jules Verne invents
A century complete with all we have
A place of material dreams

Look like upper class people
Don't care how the lower class of people live
Too poor to have a song to sing
When you gave all that you could give

III

No song
To expand his unconsciousness
As he sees each one
Like you look at them this way
So much like another
Can't quite come to mind
And they stretch, pout so charmingly then
Along graceful lines.

                    Graceful lines
Glimmering among each other's shadows
Socially.

                    She watches, coolly
As ornate old-fashioned lines
Flex through distortions
It comes between Splendora and splendor,
News from east Texas Dallas Alice

From Manhattan from Midland
From home
Soft eyes then and sudden
Hard mouths

Chit chat from strangers
Or neighbors,

Yes, they stretch out so charmingly then

IV

Glass is a shifting liquid
                    stunned by flame
          and passersby;
                    a shame
Nobody understands
Shy glass. Embarrassed buildings
Houston's pride
The city first a dream of New Yorkers
In a pickup near the icehouse
A Cajun named Jules Verne invents
A century complete with all we have
The 1950s realized at last
Views from Cody's fashion-cluttered roof
Only the most recent bent
That Graettinger & Kenton and Associates
So fervently outlined
Of Transco beacon light and boomtown press
Now and then, stinging as a Blues guitar
Muted and wan as April's palest rose.
City of glass

Glass is a shifting liquid
In disguise, bearing its panic with more grace
Than any man could ever understand
More delicate than any nervous sparrow,
Stronger than any girl's soft, yielding hand:

Here, for who wants to see it
(Though nobody asked for a sign)
Triumph of Dubuffet's "Phantom" seen
Through hurricane of Duchamp's chance
Stressed in the glass of Milam's pyramids
City of glass, a place of material dreams
Bestowed in plain sight and transparently denied.
A town where high school children on the bus
Discourse on architecture. Would-be boyfriends
Mew, "I like that new one there. You like it, too?"

Old songs from radio, ancient courting poetry and fancy talk
Magnetized here by stone striking the eye
While set designers for the TV Evening News
Frantically paste new photos on the anchorman's backdrop,
More harried than the station managers who wait for ratings

"When you show houses, you always find a way
To drive the client there along an esplanade,"
So my friend tells me. CENTURY 21 is here, unfolding
The 1950s realized at last
An awesome isometry of reflection

Facades of shining surface, blinding glass
Where the desperate mother, the unemployed man,
The brutal or blundering thief in the night
The crazies of Main Street who wander by night,
Homeless and dazed, are vanished from the frieze

Of commerce. If they were present, would be but rendered small
Glass shadows. Vampires and victims are not reflected at all.

No song

V

Those in these houses only are allowed.

This is but a gift, well-meant. This isn't gossip
Of invention, not malice.
Brightest intention, really
Something to expand
And why not what's unconscious
Since we don't know where light stars anywhere,
Just its most recent bent

There is no brilliance of subtropic sun
Today. Unseasonal. So cold, so calm.
This Gulf the radio reports so roilsome.
No gleam reflected from a murky thread
Of tainted bayou,
No brilliant humor jostling on the street
No hope, no dream coming to "save the day"
Unless you want one.

          Builded in mud, proverbial shifting sand
                    Sand fired stands still
          Long enough to qualify as glass
Banded with steel and concrete, it can touch the sky,
          A miracle.

In all this glass, when every face is seen,
These mirrors will hold conversations with the sun

We,
Chortling from babyhood to grandest dotage, sing
Each egotistic we
We sing to each awakening "Good morning"
We shout through disappointments in loud restaurants
Sleeping, we sign to ourselves.

And still
Can neither speak nor sing
What space we share or crop into coherent beauty
Here
But shards of reflection, but glimmers of shadows
No schedule but chance of annoyance,
Distracting refraction
A petulance designed of light rebounding—languid, liquid.
There is a gulf between us and ourselves
A missed perception

We need a song that all of us can sing
A true reflecting. A moody, bright, expansive song.
In all this glass, when every face is seen,
These mirrors will hold conversations with the sun.

Dancing on Main Street

. . . .

Mister Anderson
would always tell us that

if a black man
is the first
to cross your doorstep
New Year's

                you have good luck
                                all year long

        Each New Year day was
earlier eyes for him

Up & down our block
He'd go knocking
on sleepy neighbors'
                        doors

        Mister Anderson was not the sort
of man

                to leave
        his neighbors' good fortune
                up to chance

I

Any Place You've Ever Been

> *The earlier religions had their myths interpreted by means of the oral and unwritten Wisdom. We have ours* misinterpreted*; and a great deal of what has been imposed upon us as God's direct, true, and sole revelation to man, is a mass of* inverted myths, *under the shadow of which men have been cowering as timorously as birds in the stubble, when a kite in the shape of a hawk is held hovering overhead to keep them down …*
> *—Gerald Massey (1887)*

THE KITE AND THE HAWK

Man is no longer alone in the universe!

The day I found the hieroglyphic formula
For happiness for all mankind
I had to promise to give it away.

It is we have to find a way
For everyone to have
One more of something
Than your neighbor has

For you—here is a dollar!

And for you,
I feel warm brotherhood
And love intense
Beyond what anyone has ever felt before.

You didn't think I'm going around
And giving everybody money?

For me
The syllable of antique power
To shift the Light above
Enough to cast the second or third shadow
The Grand Prize
In the lottery of loneliness

SOUTH ST. BLUES

South St., you know, is not on any map.
There's just a bending line, a littered street.
It might even be a mental region.
So many faces, black, so occupied with pain and others,
just as painfully, a frozen blank.
I thought I'd crash out once (I'd seen a movie),
turned faintly philosophic, spoke at synagogues.
I'd try to talk away the taste of pigmeat
in my mouth, passing along South St. on the bus, eyes closed:
"I'm Palance dying for the thousandth time, on the
crags, name of his woman on his lips,
a letter to her, painfully writ, in his pocket. The pain
we bear before making it! Almost requisite, the
coldness, even those crags."

But Palance wouldn't do. Fugitive, I come and stroke your
hair. I smile at you. You wonder where my
eyes are. I fix my mind on you, say: "It's hard
to understand." You're only human,
want to know your stature in my eyes. Stand here, look for
my eyes, sun at your back. You'll see.
I take you without thought, trying to banish
South St. from my mind. But the days reel off like old film,
unwanted moments bang against the brain. In your
face a stolen lyric can be read, a medieval tune full
of eastern Europe, the long nights with dark
and contemplative men, the midnight pogrom.
Tune for clarinet and balalyka, violin.
You don't know why it makes me sing my kind of blues.

PLEASE, DON'T LET ME BE MISUNDERSTOOD

after Edgar Cairo

You vex me so
Impatient sigh,
Land whose liberation waits
In my own breath

Your distant yearning
Forces my conscience to protest

Word upon word
Whirls to a hurricane
Inside me

Your heavy sighs
Your whisperings
Spiral around that place
Where I must tug
Myself
To thread the sandbars of my nation's peace

My heart lists in the flood
As my blood churns

Please don't accuse me of embittered exile,
Mother. Don't call me a motherless child

WHEN IF THE BIG BANDS COME BACK

Love fills its absences with doubt
And nights with fruitless pain
Knits its brow to wring a problem
Out. Love seeds its care with rain.

Love feels departure's space
With some of the most incredible
Foolishness. Like sombreros
Purchased on a trip to Santa Fe

Greenwich Village African bracelets

Fading photographs that are mislaid
In strange places far from the place
The loved one and the lover were
Ever really together. The daily mail.

But we have to put up with it
Our most popular songs are composed
They Can't Take That Away From Me

I'll write you "Every Day I Have the Blues"

GUERRILLA GIRLS

Harbor road is handily lifted
A summer waiting in the sky
Foreigners crowd the landings
She tells me of the Nazi death camp,

Some of them the blondes feed
Me bread and safe water
And it is better than nothing.
"How you feel Joe"
She says she was born near San Reys.

Ulla's silk and rayon shift
Repeats properly
Oceans the mind busy positioning
The operation is repeated
Many times per second
Bending down beside the groaning oars
Outside the long shed

Speech,
A receiver continuously responsive and capable

Birds condense in her wool mouth
Underneath her throat knots of recognition.
Can you be busted for fucking
The enemy? The radio is curiously
Still in the tropical night

The walkie-talkie is shadowed
And morose. Just like a spring
Which released, goes beyond its usual
Position and then returns,

She releases me from politics
Inside a socialist novel
Which released, goes beyond
Its usual position and then returns, just like
That bathing suit model on the dais at Saks

DISPLACEMENT

I

To a lotus beaming in the grime

Behind the house,

The light is very clear

The parasol is painted

We moving
Guy at the
Wheel sd
"I see
They got it
Finished" But
Nothing is
Finished.

Every day someone returns
To the field

Before his wanting becomes a rainbow
He must pause.

The waters rise up
In a dull sheaf
As if miracles were due

But it is only
The harvest;
Only the buffalo's bulk
In the water

The new figure of Buddha beside the road
Between Phu Xuan and Tan Thuan Dong
Shivering in the cold
Flood of vast brown sky

II

Wish you were heir
To more naturalness
Than simple lust
For daily bread and restaurants
Where the waiters
Still speak French

Wish you could hear more
In the dark

More than crickets
Your grandfather's cough
Or the songs of
The little fishes

Listen. This is modern times all over the world
Go sit under a tree.

Who studies the physics
Of nonentities?

A facsimile becoming a disguise

Who is not supposed to be reading
This postcard

I am pleased to surprise the people
Any afternoon

And those who do not
Care to understand
That I know. You know.

Everywhere it is the same thing
Only different.
High officials
Flash by
Hostaged in their
Entourage.

She told me I'm glad
We are not important
We can go walk around
And sit in cheap
Cafés by the road.

Saigon, VNCH 1971

SENTIMENT

Grander designs for the living room paper
And the full, bright sound of the daylight
Came to touch some Thing in our thoughts
Of the misleading vacations. We blanked
And felt the force of our garments
This language that rinses in our flesh
Waterfalls coloring the air wide for identification
Our discussions at the Federal office for that
And information more irrelevant in the streets
In the end, it would only remind us
Once again the dry weekend in Boston
Hearing "Satisfaction" in the bar
Coming over the television out some
Skinny and casual illusion
The temporary grace of being in business
That the whole world surrounds
A dull sensation, like standing
Over a long empty bar drinking
Martinis at midnight just for fun
And create the unusual for Boston

Any place you have ever been still responds
To the rhythm of your illusion

REVEAL NEW INFORMATION settles there
Under the feet of the people bored
Returning from the financial world
Into soft decades of crime and world
War like a curtain across the rooms
The sane rooms. And in a room picked
At random somewhere across Boston
She is pouring water from one bowl
Into another to dye her hair gold

Where I walk in with directions and purpose
Putting slugs in cigarette machines there
Smoking and watching TV thinking abt you
This song wd be lost there in Boston,

Under my feet more startling disclosures
And I could go on singing almost forever!

Of course not.

Until that song falls down

There is nothing
So beautiful

The form of artifice destroys itself
Axxxx xxx xfxxx xxxxxxxxxx rx xxxx
xxxxxxxx xxxx xxxxx it is as if you
Had stolen away to the river some calm
(Good!) but the river was flushing 300 red-
Faced conventioneers to the Falls

And cared to do nothing about this!

Thinking: it will be good for at least half
A page in the scrapbook you misplaced

DREDGE RIVER FOR CONVENTION BODIES

Thinking it will be worth six good words
Over dinner of baked macaroni and meat-
Balls with a mushroom and onion gravy sauce
And black coffee served in classical cups

I am ashamed of that Good. The slow down trip
The mirrors of a music box settled
On "The Inventions" some such golden
Racket annoyance lace organic satins

Pink bunched up around the doll
Who sits in the album and
Worries about the sunlight
Of years already forgotten

Lost in the old corners of deshabille peasant
Evenings with the same old wallpaper and
Same old dull slide show white boys meet
White girls at the Charles white bicycles

Washed by the elegant light playing it up and
Flicker in the room where a woman
Puzzles her mirror with the chemical dream
Turning herself into a photo of old Boston

What you said, and almost collapsing back into the rum

And the sky so open this morning
No such thing as the Mediterranean
Only the smell of trees in Boston
Sunlight in her new ridiculous hair
Under my feet. More startling disclosures.
And I could go on singing almost forever!

Of course not.

SUBURBAN SATURDAYS

Given choices, standing in the street
And shouting
Even for a worthy cause
The way we used to do
When we were young
Even for nothing
Is not choice

The world has changed.

Homely estrangements
In the presence of one's children
Is more fun
Less public and, embarrassing to say, less private
Even.
                    You're weeping through
The Way We Were on cable
They are saying, "Huh?
I don't like Barbra Streisand anyway
Her nose is funny"
                              They have no time for you
No words and infinitely less concern
They vanish after dark
Just like you taught them to at 3
But now it hurts.
All parents reach this point, a cliff.
Maturity is what we like to call it

The world has changed
Manners your elders strapped you into
Somehow have come unraveled in your hands
You watch the loose ends
Flap away like thoughtless tongues
Dances, movies, parties

Impudent and bold, and beautiful
And realize, that given choices,
Had you known,
It really wouldn't have turned out this way

MORNING RAGA

While you slept undoubtedly
Some tragedy occurred
And the dismal muezzins
Of the half-past modern
Western world begin to chatter
Powdered and grave
Wrapping the world
In a one-size-fits-all demise
Provided for promotional considerations

But somewhere someone
Is watching *Orphée Noir*
Thinking Jobim is wonderful
And thinking how great it must be
To believe someone must sing
A song to bring the sun
Up

While those happily tangled hesitate
Confusing duty with a slow myopic scanning
Of the single face
That captures all the brand-new light
Releasing it one eyelash at a time

As students giggle riding on a train through Tyrol
Missing islanded monasteries from the guidebook
But not the real smell of sheep and swine
Beside the roadbed as the train slows down
Sliding into and out of flowered little towns

And somewhere where it is already yesterday
Or still tomorrow
In just a little while
Someone will say:

While you slept undoubtedly
Some tragedy occurred
If you think you'll be happier
That way, starting your day
Believe them

But some
Where some
One is
Singing.

THE AUDIE MURPHY GAME

When I was an infant playing
With myself I dreamed of Fame

Being an infantry hero being in movies
Recounting my patriot murders
Playing myself. Drunkenly driving
To death if need be to fulfill

This legend in my own time. Tsk tsk.
When I discovered I could not
Win the Vietnam war I couldn't
Be a hero dammit I couldn't wear

The Congressional Medal of Honor
I was very disappointed. I cried
To the gods for a second chance

And the gods cried back "no way buddy"

II

Rituals and Improvisations

DESTRUCTION OF THE SEATED MAN

after De Kooning's Seated Man, *ca. 1938, now destroyed*

I

bloodless hands glowing
staring at each other's emptiness
postured as if expecting
something to hold
wistful apprehension
the lines of the face
could be disbelief fascination?
suspended fear maybe anxiety
of impending whirlwinds
the boiling shadows
eat at the flesh
and shining hands too weak
to grasp eternity
wait for it to fall into their
upturned palms.

II

perhaps those eyes are
watching some color splashed smeared
abstraction of the Landing
or the silent cool night-beauty—
sky lit with a distant neon rainbow
watching the vermilion montage of morning
rape the trembling nightness

III

the penetrating darts
through the shoulders
later tore off the shadow-bitten

head sent it spinning thru the
electrified landscapes of Death
the man still sat in the bright vacantness
some of us can make our world
blackwhite and sit headless with waiting hands
forever

LAST CALL

In *The Odyssey*, Book IX, we learn of a fierce battle with the Ciconians on the island of Ismaros:

> From that place we sailed onward much discouraged, but glad to have escaped death, although we had lost good companions. Yet we did not let the galleys go off, until we had called thrice on the name of each of our hapless comrades who died in that place.
> —*The Odyssey*, tr. W. H. D. Rouse

Erwin Rohde, in *Psyche*, comments: "References to similar callings upon the dead in later literature make the meaning of such behaviour clear. The souls of the dead who have fallen in foreign lands must be 'called'; they will then, if this is properly done, follow the caller to their distant home, where an 'empty grave' awaits them."

This poem is about veterans of the war in Viet Nam.

> *"If anybody's carrying a rabbit's foot, hang on to it tight."*
> *—Van Johnson, in* 30 Seconds Over Tokyo

Corned beef sandwiches, water, plenty
Of time to think about the future
You too can grow up to be a square-jawed
American hero, eyes rounding up with recognition
That horror that looked so darn familiar
Really knows you. Grew up in the same town
And memorized the same stupid movies.
It's just us now, huddled in the same apprehension
That whatever is outside this bubble
Is probably no stranger. It gets harder
To swallow, the temperature's rising,
The lies and the half-truths go whistling by

Stand by
For voices blending into stridency
Practiced as alarms
This is the daily danger

We would stay awake,
Missing nothing. Clear the head.
There is some place now

Just as it materializes on this page
Or fills the ear of the peaceful sleeper

Familiar
As a song that has been on the radio
About six weeks, the smile a little grayer
But the same no-nonsense haircut,
And the words of the heartbroken girl
Making sense. Suddenly, clear the head!

It's me Clothilde!

What are you afraid of? The fires behind us
Are our signatures. Our memories cannot harm us,
Unless we allow them to talk to our friends
And anyone who'd believe them is not really a friend.

Oh poo, she teases.
You have been lax
Don't you remember me
Your pretty little America
Blue and shimmering

Around the corner is a warm and cozy place
Complete with lovable and laughing folks
Waiting in a kind of strange suspenseful animation
For us. To just appear and be ourselves is all
They live for. Anticipation of our beauty
Keeps them lifelike, poised, waiting for your call.
You see? These are your memories.
They will say what you want them to say
And amuse you. They will whine and cower,
Backbite you into the most heartless, unfeeling
Wretch the world has ever known
The most untrustworthiest son of a bitch

The most thankless, loving serf of humanity
Most sweetest, kindest, cut-throat whatever
Until you are happy. See? What are friends for?

Let's get it on before big sister comes.
We dare not admit even suspicions of failure
It is better not to even begin.
And no time wasted on remember when.
I think the truth might be a little prettier
With a bit of stainless steel and neon
Over here. Maybe some glass bricks.
A miniature rain forest in the bath
Sounds a lot better than pipes that drip all night

Our hearts are blessed with an efficient fancy
Corned beef sandwiches, water, plenty
Reasons to be happy in love. So we didn't know
Where we were going, but we are finally here!
A carnival of soft-spoken meanness
Welcomes you to your new refrigerator carton
And honored place among the lowest middle-class

Gee, you look so familiar

EXCITATION

O wondrous thing it is
Oh what a wondrous thing it is
We often thought, to live
Through the senses
When they quicken and stir at even

One
Assays kaleidoscopes of failing light
Another
Revels in the moist kiss of the night
Approaching

                    soon enough chased,
The kiss, by the dry scentlessness of central heat
So Prussian, so precise

                              When nature struggles against artifice
In a madly sensuous pas de deux
Lovely as the chevrons of late traffic
Dancing across high ceilings, cooling walls
Fleeting to sight yet permanent
In the mind's storage place of kinetics
To be unwrapped some day when words fail
And, like any forgotten bundle in a warehouse
Puzzling because no one remembers what they were
What use they serve
Where did this stuff come from?
Or even how the hell it got here
Such simple-minded mysteries can make your day

ALL OF THIS IS A CERTIFIED EXCERPT FROM A DREAM.
  THERE WERE SPIRITS
HOVERING OVER OR AS IN THE OLD LANGUAGE'S SIGNS
  "UP ABOVE MY HEAD"

A SPECIAL SORT OF MUSIC IN THE AIR . . . SOMETHING THAT
WAKES YOU UP
JUST LIKE SUNLIGHT
LIKE A PHONECALL AT DAWN
15 MINUTES BEFORE THE ALARM GOES OFF
A ROUGH AND ROLLING MUSIC
LIKE 1940S BLUES
WHISKEY & WOMEN AND ALL THE OTHER JIVE
THE JIVERS KNEW
ALL THE SINGERS OF SENSE WHO HAD NO SENSE
OR ELSE THEY WOULDN'T HAVE BEEN SINGING
"WELL, YOU KNOW . . ."

The permutations,   or
just   listening
Roscoe Gordon
Peppermint
"I Been Booted"
or is it "... just got"
FAT GIRL BOOGIE
& sordid ordered trash
The permuted sounds
of a special estranged English
And who in hell
and this is it, if nowhere else
will ever ever understand
That all of these cats
were Charles Brown
yes, even
Nat "King" Cole
urbane and suave
his pictures in the best of *JET*
In those pulp days, pulp times
A hundred years past slavery still
The same old shuffle
In Alabama, where the redneck fans
attacked poor Nat on stage   just like Roland Hayes
knocked him down, down to the ground
sd, "Nigger!"

Such raw country voices, the Ku Klux Klan meets Rhythm & Blues

IT SOUNDS LIKE THIS:

Byebye, bye
Baby
byebye
Oh what a wondrous thing
I think it is
But goddam baby
baptist to the heart
I'm getting tithed of you, momma
But I love, Lord knows
most as much as I loves
myself

AND LOST LOTS OF FOOLS
MOANING & GOING ON (in the background)

Certainly, this should awaken the mind
And the senses should shut down in shame
But it is such a lovely clear break in the day
Only a fool who would remain a fool
Would have the nerve to shoo this shoofly away

"Anytime you bother me, bubba . . ."
But, momma,
You
Can bother the heck
Out of me!

If you were me
Or anywhere
by me
Or near,
Baby baby baby
What a scene this cd be here
Oh baby baby baby
And lots of lost fools
Moaning & going on (way in the background y'know)

Just like church   way back
in the wildwood
just like in the arbor
somewhere just outside
And lost fools
just like church   way back
in the wildwood

moaning & going on
like in de brush arbor
somewhere just outside
up   down
back of town

So much to say, we negroes here
Oh yes, we've had some fun
Have sang the blues and did what had to be done
We often thought, to live
O what a wondrous thing
Fleeting to sight yet permanent
To sit despised on the outskirts of your town
Black flat deprived & jap-eyed
Yes, we sing. "Baby baby baby, why you?"
When nature struggles against artifice
To be unwrapped some day when bullshit fails
And, like any forgotten bundle in a warehouse
Lovely as the chevrons of late traffic
So Prussian, so precise
Like a phonecall at dawn from your baby
Moaning & going on . . .
Such simple-minded mysteries can make your day

The jivers knew
All all of these acts
Were Charles Brown's
A rough and rolling music
Just like sunlight
Just like Church

Fleeting to sight yet permanent
To be unwrapped some day
When words fail
What use they serve
Or else they wouldn't have been
Singing

SKUNK INSULATION

Random
As any Oklahoma
Rundown
As a long black silence
Roadway
Slicing vacancies
And separations
U.S. Highway metronome
Into tick-thuds
Of wheels on asphalt

All a formal invitation to the jolt

You can roll up the windows
                                        don't work
Light up a Camel
                                        don't work
Believe I say, do you BELIEVE
In even a roadkill Heaven
Where there's never
Any traffic anymore
To fan and flutter your
Conscience swooning ease
                                    won't work
Act tough
Until
The tears burst
From your ears
                                        will do no good

No brutish plan, no choice of sin
Can tip a karmic scale
No euphemisms of passion
Or vampired politeness
Could make any difference,

For 2.5 miles or 3 minutes
You could
Hold your breath
Try for a record
or simply admit it

Nothing gives up this world
Without a comment

GRUDGE MATCH

Mocking as sunrise
To insomniacs
As painfully predictable
Is a resentful child
Who boldly signs her mother's malady
Wishing a womb again
Curls into silences
And flames with mute disdain
Her empty-headedness
Provides a constant echo
Of Dad's failures

A healthy family might shout
And rage their way through this
To an embrace of sanity.
At least, civility.
A wealthy one would pack her off to school
Hoping
That somewhere in a corner of this earth
Another pair has built a boy
To match this fool

LIFELONG LEARNING

One day my Dad
Decided
Whatever else we were in life
We should be rich

I don't like being poor
He said, I don't like
Getting up at 4 o'clock dark
Day after day
2 subways to somebody's job
To put 3 dollars every week
Into a Christmas club
And after scrimp and save and all

What come
The end of every month
The same rob Peter
To pay Paul

There's got to be a better way

The scheme he fell for was a scam
"Direct mail"
Was the road we chose
To riches

We sent away for
Mailing lists, ordered a crate of doohickeys
Printed 1,000 flashy ads
Return address embossed
The name we picked
H. HAMILTON RICKARD & SONS
Would sound to suckers like we'd been
In business for a century

"Purveyors of fine doohickeys"

We didn't do so well
Of course
A small fortune in stamps was lost
By Christmas
No cash left to shop
We did the best
With what we'd got:
Doohickeys went to all our friends

What never broken never mends

OTIS

Some women think
A man should hunt for them

Some women understand it

And some men think
Return a wondrous thing

She must be waiting

The dude goes out,
Is gone all night
She knits and yearns
Till gray dawnlight
Her girlfriends say,
"That trifling
                    blank
Ain't coming back"
And help her undo her
                                        work

That's the kind of cat,
You know,
"No man can take
My place"
Instantly trucks his shadow
Through the door
Catches a fit
That blinds him
Even further.

Folks like that
You hear about them
On the News.

Some women understand it

Another dude,
You know,
Is gone for days
But she sits, humming
At first a moan
She knits and polishes
And frets.
She frowns at friends
Then sings a gleeful song
As they fidget them
Whisper, "Girl,
Is you gone mad?"
So all of them chorusing
"That trifling
                    blank
Um hmmm, I knows
                              a man!"

Some women
Man, by the time
My man tipped in
She had damn near enough
Macramé string
To make a hammock
That sleep two
                    on top
Three on the
                  bottom

Some women
                    think
And there is beauty
In the knit
              of thinking

Some dudes know
How to treat a woman
Right

Some don't

Some women understand it

SPIRITS YOU ALL

The Charles Gayle Trio at the Houston Jazz Festival, September 16, 1992

for Charles Gayle

All it is

Church

If you hear it

He
Church

He
Concerthall flame breath
To sidewalk
Breathes
Through a saxophone
To deep pulsing tunnels
The people
Whipped by the money changers
Beat down by money
Hang wearily
Awaiting darkness
Bats

He church
Speaking no words
Their souls are not silent
He
Makes audible
The sonar of thousands
The horn coaxes measured Jesus
Sing
Gayle,
Angular

Erect
Vattel Cherry dances
Bass
Bells like the click of cowries
Flash like sparks
Around his instrument
Marc
Edwards reaches
For a distant drumbeat
Snaring it, then lets
It go
To fly around this space

Inside his saxophone
Are all the voices
Spirits you all
The shrieks of Daddy Grace
And grandmaw's moan

Young girls
All that is truly precious of the earth
Loud and laughing
Who do not know
The troubles of this world
Glowing
With bells in their ears
Fluttering bird-like
In girl conspiracies

From concerthall under red lights
To sidewalks exiled from neon

If you can hear it
Spirits you all
Dance from this saxophone

Cold light in falling darkness

Under the shudder of Suburbans
Fuming on the overpass
A woman in a carton
She might have asked a husband
To break down
And stack beside the drive for heavy trash
Busies her hands
Folding rags with gracious care
Into a plastic bag

Her heart just idles
And her mind curls up
Around a picture of a small white clapboard
Missionary Baptist Church
Nestled in hope beside a county road
Where the choir voice
Was all the sound of life
To laughing girls
And soft brown faces
Some of them softened only
When they sang

Church don't mean religion
May even be a verb

Sleeping in fits
A man ten feet away
Wrapped in a sheet of cardboard
Does not dream;
That lobe was leached
In floods of liquid flame
That made 1,000 nights like this
Instant forgettings
And survivable
He does not see himself
In marcelled hair
Long gleaming Stacy Adams cordovans
As dangerous as German U-boats

On the Dreamland floor
As the orchestra
High trumpet, hoarse trombones
Slides into “Cherry Pink
And Apple Blossom White”

You think these cracked feet
Have no mambo memory?
Well, no they don’t
He never did that
But he saw it in a movie once
A century ago

He
Church in trembles

Joy?

And struggle
Jjjoy and and struggle

Here
Where night’s a cloak
Of heavy hopelessness
And day a flash of puzzled patterns
Lining it
A fashion
Such ill-fitting materiality
That even those who grab the most
See themselves scrambling
To barely cover their behinds

And now the brazen shofar of a horn
As the commuter bats
Unfold themselves into
The evening
And step along the sidewalk
And do not look around or down

And if they do don't see
What you can hear
Spiraling out of Charles Gayle's saxophone
Spirits you all

Know where it comes from

Church if you feel it

JOURNEY OF 1,000 LI

It's as if all my memory
Is still on decks of cards

Everyone else has chips
Shuffled carelessly

Blue-backed diamonds ending up
In a red deck

Where I expected Christmas 1949 to be
Phone numbers

Though "Sunday Morning" always is
Exactly where it's always been

It's playing havoc with my *Pensées*
Which ought to be

Bright insights based on turns
Of clever sayings

Polished to delight
By life's experiences

What never dims, though
Is your specialness

Beloved, if we were in China
I'd owe you my life

Or is it have to teach you
How to fish

TIRADE

Now I know old age is cruel
It brings fears you never knew

There is a hazard in the morning sun,
A thirty percent chance
This day will pass without
The birth of a regret
Or the blossoming of a sorrow
So well behaved and mild
Shyly, patiently
Gaining courage all these years
Blurting into the bliss
You've sown around you

These passions make your life last longer
Waiting for the day
You can no longer push them away.
Arms weakened,
Your heart grows stronger
And wisdom clinging to you like a child
To her broken doll,
You may finally sort everything out
And end with nothing
Left to fear tomorrow

III

The Simplest of All Mysteries

POEM IN LIEU OF THE MARRIAGE OF ANDREW ZOLEM

We met like songs say in a cellar café
Maybe we were sad   we were smoking
Thinking of your living room flowery laughter
And the ladies coming by to play mah-jongg

To have been brought up here, a house with books
And someone vaguely remembering great music
During unusual moments when pruning the hedge
Gallantly shuffling toward the new bed

He takes off the dark cape-like robe revealing
Black silk pajamas   Leaps tenderly into
The white folds of the bridge and thinks and
Comes, is it the harlot of "Claire de Lune"

Is it the tacky innocence of Debussy now waking up now
Here on the chest and the arms of the custom
Where the recent past returns, the rear guard of
The white flowers serenades and card games

Blackjack in the fat parlor after her family
Had gone to bed. Softly touching his hand
When it was her turn to deal   Or playing whist
Trump trump   pawed over the small table.

Then the parents would come in with their lies
Or cough from their sloppy insomniac bed
Thinking of her sluffing it off at breakfast
Don't you think I know you know I care

The table with the two different death services
Livery and tambourines on the one hand
Even though she lived in a bourgeois comm-
Unity built on the expected assent

We ignore when these white designs are brought to the room
And evil marriage, virtuous as a lab attendant
Comes up out of the photograph just like "La Mer"
Out of all the white vases like soft dallying

Which is not literature or the social structure
Which is not the province of the first night
Now, now sleep reigns contrary to the caveat
Emptor of our Jewishness and careful instructions

We realize that we are no longer aware of Spain
Its sunlight and love songs. Our wedding
Night has been unnecessary like no songs say.
With your ring we have aborted our children

And our youth shuffles toward the dusty encyclopedia
That we will have to buy them, toward sex books
You will find under their pillows   tsk tsk
The theme of Faro explains your lover's death

It is all there, cached in your stupid new husband.
Children will dig it up to sell you subscriptions
You could have had those beautiful, sly little bastards
Know it, Orpheus sends back your regards.

THE SADNESS OF SPACE EXPLORATION

for Karen

We must never grow up
If all we learn is kindness

Not making promises
We may not know how to keep
Is both affection and an immaturity
That baffles feelings
Amid the circus clamor
Of a pleasant village day
Humid with rituals and schoolkids

Because passion is a need beyond desire
His matinee-style courtliness
Is matched by her astonished grace

Two gleeful children hide in them
Under the shadows of heaven
Deciphered and confused again
Beneath fidgeting trees.

QUIET RIOT

I'd rather not negotiate
An understanding

I have no taste
For anorexic conversations
Without your richly-layered innuendo
Or parables of just desserts
Among acquaintances

If you really have something to say
It's worth breaking out the good china

Put the damn tin cup away

DUMB LUCK

Because
I could not fix my mouth to say
I need you so
You saw me coming

When you have lived so long
Your only prayer
Is Lord, please
Give me one more clear
Indignity to magnify
That length of suffering
Becomes the latest fashion
With transatlantic fortunes riding
On a hem,

In the moon-rinsed
Casinos of romance
I gamed and lost.

Wrong choice
Of games.
Stammers
Of pride

And 3 unanswered hearts
No time left
For the simple dice-toss
Of a plain apology.
And, in the end
I could not raise a hand
Against you

THE NEW SOUTH

A sentimental drunkard
Don't you know
"Cottage For Sale"
3 a.m. Vegas lonely standard time
Brought me to tears

Impoverished no way
Except mementos
Daydream afternoons
Of make-believe old age
And modest wealth

The way things ought to be

I lusted for the luxury
Imagine
To have a shuttered witness
To a year we lived on Art and lentils
Joyously

In (of all places) Pine Bluff, Arkansas
The house we loved in
Owned by a cracked belle
Who had the place torn down
The month we moved

An attitude
Just a little more extreme
Than your own mother's
Who only said, Make sure
You don't keep grass around the house

You two have enough problems

LIGHTS OUT

It's not that I've grown blind
To your attractions
Or that your beauty
Is enhanced by candlelight
The way Frank Capra
Rubbed petroleum jelly on the lens
To make us yearn
Until a held breath
Clenches our hearts
For Barbara Stanwyck

But, as you say
It's not that how we feel
About each other is so new
Or special like it has never
Been an overworked cliché
Happened to us or anyone
Before (even in movies)
But, really very simply
Diminishing distractions
Never hurts

NO, DON'T GET UP

I watched her throw
Her ribbons on the floor
She put her foot down.
I asked her, as she turned
Toward the door
"Where will you go?"
"Crazy," she answered
"And I insist on driving myself."

THE FAILURE OF ALCHEMY

What love accounts for
In this day and time
Trusted somewhat less than safety

A bond that ensures

Tears
Even if counterfeit
Earn interest

Yet and still

There comes a day
Weary of starving greed
True love goes blind

And leaves a wife who could be good

Stumbling through chores
Vacuuming his pockets
Heart and mind.

WORKING-CLASS HERO

Some days feels like
You wake up underwater
It isn't the humidity I'm talking about

Space folds on space. A blue icehouse.
And every motion climbs into itself
A little man in someone else's overcoat

Some days are Sunday all day long
Below an empty sky that's eyeball blue
A slight wind curling round you like a vine

A day to put your bag on the conveyor belt
And walk on through

What kind of day today?
You could just say
I really didn't need something
To tell my grandkids

THE GAMBLER

Took a note on my house in Ozone Park
That's why I'm out here working
I don't need to be out here you know
I did something I know I shouldn't do
Gave 27,000 to my kids

The boy's OK,
Though.
Smooth as Chinese silk
A engineer
Married to a Philadelphia gal
My wife don't care
For her, but she's OK

My girl's in school getting a masters
That's why I'm out here working

That girl,
I knew it from the first
My son's little girl, too

They was born to break hearts

KNIGHT TO QUEEN'S PAWN

I married you because
You said you
Loved to cook
A gamelan of 3rd grade mischief
In your voice enchanted me
And I was hungry.

I married you
Because you swore to God
You were blond all over

Well
Your wealthy uncle
Who was set to croak
At any minute
Is now 112 years old

Your promises are dulled by overuse
And neither of us has set hearts-a-singing

Still
If we have nothing left
But carnal beauty

Well, I can live with that

AN OLD HAND

Life's not
A puzzle not a game
Eventually you learn
A thing or two
You should have known
When you were 20

        Woman content with nothing

A bad deal

        You'll find the hardest job you ever had
Is coming home

It's tough being enough

PORNOGRAPHY = EXPLOITATION OF MEN

Homework for husbands
Who remain somehow devoted
To the proposition
It is possible to satisfy 40ish women
In a childish culture
Perhaps well-chosen small appliances
Can do what major purchases
                                        have ceased to do

These men spend avid hours
Friday nights
Behind dim Main St. doors
With loosened neckties
                                taking careful breaths
Cruising the aisles
Of video arcades
Blindingly lit hoards
Of modern marvels of communication
Where no one speaks
                            more than half a dozen words
Amid shelves stacked
                            with produce
From sex factories
                        of Florida and California
Small cities in between
Send forth the works
Of amateurish Adams homely Eves
Do-it-yourself de Sades
Efforts that prove
                        anything in life
With enough effort
                        can be made boring

Jussive or stupefying calisthenics
Offering the emptiest of promises

Invitations to imagine
What has just been actually seen
Is what it is

Not idolatry of flesh
But desperate
Pursuit of possibility denied
By what's already possessed
Is what moves them

Not a prayer
But certainly a wish
So fervent
It jars the deep tectonics of desire
Beyond the boundaries
                                        of a solitary mind
Beyond the limits
                                of this single flesh

A banquet for one withering belief
100 percent American
                                    and truly human
If anyone has done it
                                    anything can be done
These men spend money for nothing
Safe sex on the edge
                                  of sad discretion

Here are lust's bargains

Movies for men
Who after 20 years
On the same job
Half of their friends laid off
Have modest wants:

Enough to pay the bills
And some left over

A wife who still glows in the dark

NOW YOU CAN WORRY

Tonight she's wearing her rejection slip
A plotted frumpiness

O you don't know the pain
To look into the midnight eyes
Of that little child
In that picture from El Salvador
That total silence
That premature despair
And feel you can do nothing
Nothing you can do

Tonight she feels so frustrated
She almost cries

I've put up with that woman
For three years
You'd have been proud of me
I didn't turn all black, you know
All red eyeballs, "Now listen Bitch!"
Instead I did it
Like that Larry Davis song
You used to like
"Walk Out Like a Lady"
But I did tell her
Where to put her job

I mean it seems so hopeless
So deeply meant but somehow also false
Crying about retarded whales
Dim-witted dolphins hunting tuna
Who wind up horrifyingly in salads

Sometimes you wonder
Think how the whole world
Is just going to hell
Not just this neighborhood and this house
The *environment*
A world with just
The darkest colors of the rainbow left
As if we try but just can't do enough
God knows, I try.
But anyway, I've decided
To do the little I can do

No sex for you

L'ARGENT

I know you don't know what
Love is it isn't
Dagwood kisses on the way to work
It's going to work

Love could be but it's not
A 50/50 partnership
Matched sets of polished lies
A usury of affection

I understand that you don't understand
Money don't grow on trees

And if it did,
Those trees would grow
So far away
It would be work to get it

IV

Resistance as Memory

THINKING IN WORDS

Instead of meat
Or any of several barometrically
Possible expressions of fluids
Produced out of flesh, we are drenched
With an intoxicating sympathy
As wonderful as a show business awards banquet

Perhaps in more private
Self-congratulation
We might sit in paneled rooms
And toast ourselves
In Perrier or schnapps

Thinking in strong but well-scrubbed Germanic
Words adopted by romantic conversation
Knowledge of their natural parents lost
To counterfeit a long melodious decay
We might call Art or serious concern

Say, "homeless"

To a young man like me is adventure
Tasty as a bar-b-que sandwich
Melted fat thick on my fingers,
Lips glistening
Pungent aroma curling
Through my whiskers
Thinking up pretty names for the wind
Flirting in the top of oaks across the field
Or swirling in angry like Barbara Stanwyck

Yes—I could call the wind "Barbara"
Or "Miss Stanwyck"
                                        No, "Babe"
Now, you can imagine that

Say in urine perception
Bringing us nose up to piss
With the waste of fellow humans?

Wouldn't your lip curl away—
Freedom fighter, weirdo, wino,
Heart-rending refugee or mental case
Only seen clear
When we're properly thinking
In words

So the distinction can be made
Between bar-b-qued felons
And napalmed bystanders
We need to be thinking in words
To tell our hearts and minds
Which way to flutter

As the song says: "No fear, no shame"
As the song says: "Ain't no mountain high enough"
As we scale an Everest of thoughtful
Good intentions, shapely spandex consciences
A myriad glittering categories dancing

Toward a happy day
When nothing liquid or greasy is left
Uncontaminated by our kindness
Once accurately defined
No human
                left untampered with
No slimy duck
                unturned. And laundered.

LIKE A TREE

for Kwaku Pierce

I

The gleaners roll in
With heaped shopping carts

We have constructed ruins
To be reborn out of

Here in our cities, a question
Is there life after birth

II

Cynical innocents
Who think knowledge is dope
Facing the future
With resentful faces
& battery-operated
Primitive art

Throat-slitting music
Martial anthems
For a war on drugs
That scoops up teenage alchemists
Who cook up crack
Who conjure up themselves
Lost

No distant mountainsides, no midnight airdrops
Just sad chumps getting busted on the hottest TV show
Since Allen Funt

III

There is no vanishing point in our art
Ancestors do not go away
You say they are here
It is not even a question
Of return

Silent and dynamic
A gleaming symmetry of ancestral faces
Smooth African puzzle
That tested
Renaissance mathematics

Ebony or mahogany
Chosen because it is the living color of a man
Matched to the wood carver's own hand

The art is how to
Recognize the spirit
Is the thing you see
These wooden faces looking out
Are not portraits
They are the beings
Who were visiting that tree
When Kwaku found it

SIGHTSEEING IN EAST TEXAS

These towns are orphans of the Interstate
A slow-motion beauty
Often fires these town squares
With sparks of homely pride
Marvelous stately oaks
Or bright and loved azaleas
Accenting solid buildings
From the 1880s
Which keep, somewhere within,
Bound yellowed scraps
Of what this place has been
That nothing in the Courthouse
Parking slips filled with new cars
Dust-plated pickup trucks
And small-town silences
Even provides a whispered hint
Once happened here

What kind of folks could watch and cherish
Memories of seeing
A man nailed to a tree
Of crimes not hidden in the dark
But planned as carefully with glee
As county fairs or picnics
Hearing wept prayers
And piercing screams turn to mute shock
Brisk bidding sweeps the crowd
For toes and fingers, ears
As flames of hatred
Eddy around numb feet
Then catch a kerosene-soaked cuff
And suddenly,
A human form of flesh and soul
Is drowned in fire?
Just us.

Don't think too long
Buckle up your seat belt
And drive on.
We have survived a history that proves
That people, not necessarily humans
Can live without hearts

PSALM

et je suis triste, Signeur, d'être si triste.
—Blaise Cendrars

This morning, cold
Somewhere beyond a single mockingbird
I heard again
A haunting Negro song
Were you there when
They crucified my Lord?

After a decade
Of felons in high places,
Greed unleashed
To herd us into Hell

We're all there now
For lesser crucifixions.

Just another wet East Texas day
Dawn scrubs the sky from darker to light gray

I don't know what to do
I don't know what to do

And all our journalists declare
"The world is mad!"
The same who cried
The end of history in all the streets
The same who yelled "Surf's up!
Democracy is cresting like a tidal wave"
Bringing its flood of common oddities
To all the world
Declare, "The world is mad!"
And have no trouble finding testaments
Rumors, portents and signs
Our people lost in hearts of deserts
Our cities falling from within

Warm valleys white with flames of uprising
Tricksters and traitors
Posing as candidates but well prepared
To fall back on careers
As foul-mouthed comics

We're in the tube, my friends

I don't know what to do
Lord, I don't know what to do

In Kampuchea and South Africa
In middle Europe, Yeats's Ireland, Los Angeles, Somalia
Boys are initiated into death
Before they learn the skill that brought them here

Children completely dipped in numbing pain
Conduct a routine slaughter in the streets
Of innocents and others just like them
Kidnapped into a mindless helical design

I don't know what to do, Lord
I don't know what to do

Here on a slate-gray morning
A cold front comes up from the hill country
Bringing chill rain
Lawmen in 4 × 4s and helicopters
The crack Booze, Butts and Bombs detail
Our square-jawed champions
Until they bite the dust
When suddenly transformed
Soft family men, the best of us
And there's a fund to help
The family

Psychotic prophets
Without the foresight to have booked
A *Passion Play*

End up in re-enactment of the Alamo
A muddy siege
Each dawn both sides count heads and feet
Beneath the thudding racket
Of a sky filled with our journalists
In traffic helicopters

This frenzied Passover
Confused with Lent
Catches our breaths like wind
And clouds our faces

If not for a woman's hand,
Peace officers, pacing in high-tech tents
Would send a hundred people to the grave
For bypassed payment of their bullet fees
In carnage more insane than Attica

Thank you for this, O Lord

Thank you O Lord
For the comfort of minute awareness
Our journalists have not forsaken us
Return to tell in microwave Homerics
A vigil that disrupts
The Price Is Right each morning
Just before the Showcase Showdown
But cuts away
Before we miss the end
Who wins the game.

A little charity is what we need
And there's a fund
For pro-life murderers
And funds for milk
Where childhoods blaze and infancies implode
Upon a bed of cinders
Reflected in the dark, round
Always and forever open eyes

Of those made homeless, hopeless
By bombs and guns made in the USA
Properly taxed
Or smuggled by collusion of the law
And slushfund patriots

O Lord, I don't know what to do
I don't like watching what comes into view
I will narrow my eyelids
Till there is nothing in the world but You

Waco, Texas, 1993

BACK IN THE DAY

When we were boys
We called each other "Man"
With a long *n*
Pronounced as if a promise

We wore felt hats
That took a month to buy
In small installments
Shiny Florsheim or Stacy Adams shoes
Carried our dancing gait
And flashed our challenge

Breathing our aspirations into words
We harmonized our yearnings to the night
And when old folks on porches dared complain
We cussed them out
        under our breaths
And walked away
        and once a block away
Held learned speculations
About the character of their relations
With their mothers

It's true
That every now and then
We killed each other
Borrowed a stranger's car
Burned down a house
But most boys went to jail
For knocking up a girl
He really   truly   deeply   loved
    really   truly   deeply

But was too young
Too stupid, poor, or scared
To marry

Since then I've learned
Some things don't never change:
The breakfast chatter of the newly met
Our disappointment
With the world as given

Today,
News and amusements
Filled with automatic fire
Misspelled alarms
Sullen posturings and bellowed anthems
Our scholars say
Young people doubt tomorrow
This afternoon I watched
A group of young men
Or tall boys
Handsome and shining with the strength of futures
Africa's stubborn present
To a declining white man's land
Lamenting
As boys always did and do

Time be moving on
Some things don't never change
And how
back in the day
Well
things were somehow better

They laughed and jived
Slapped hands
And called each other "Dog"

WHALE SONG

You just don't know
How hard it is
To be uncivilized

You think that everyone you eat
Deserves to be eaten

Lunch for me
Means someone ain't coming home

So what
If breakfast might have been
The tuna that found a cure for cancer?

Damn sure was tasty!

SONGS WITHOUT SHADOWS

It's very good, black brother,
that you sing when you're in doubt.
—Nicolás Guillén

One day
A million years ago
Someone awoke
And found
That sweat and laughter
Had deserted an old friend
The only thing
The desperately still alive
Could do
Was coax the corpse into a fetal Q
And place it in a pit
Hoping to fool some magic
Into thinking their gone friend
Was ready to be born

A lot has happened since
But on this score
There seems to have been no progress
For a million years or more:

We're waiting

■

One day
Out of a clear blue sky
She says
Our life is at
A crossroads
Our future's
In our hands

Her face was businesslike
But behind her eyes
There was a loaded magazine of tears
She got up and ran to the phone

Collecting estimates for home repairs

■

One day and one day
After another
Dumb, puzzled rage
I watched my country incinerate my countrymen
In Philadelphia, on a black Mayor's word
City that bears friendship's name
Chorillo shattered
Under pretext of el General's
Illegitimate arrest
Waco, Texas, a few miles from where I live
We watched a televised apocalypse

How can this be? Where will it end?

■

Stupidity and greed, the right and left hands
Of a bogus god called Power
Hold us in stern embrace,
Have lashed the world onto a spinning wheel
Of ever more accelerated pain

As if there were surprises
The personality's addiction reappears
Cloud-like simplicity
What can be seen in a face or figure
At the start of all highways
Of songs without shadows,
Of spoken love erasing poetry,
I stand and watch my step

We have mistaken for a possibility our deepest need:
Strength in a woman that is
Soft and warm the natural
Manifold and maybe infinite
Capacity in men for lifelong
And immediate devotion
And have no songs that even whisper
This
Only the din and clatter of a desperate rush
To capture life in the stink of the moment
And hang it in the market-stall for a quick sale

■

Once I started walking to Saigon
And found a tiny village marketplace
Where an old woman displayed shining things
I left there with a bag of bargains
Viciously bartered candlesticks and platters
Beautifully wrought, melted and hammered
Marvelously shaped from spent shell casings
Made in the USA
That would make lovely presents for my aunts

Each mile I walked, shirt melted to my skin
Was marked by one more treasure left beside the road

I am just a wanderer
I've told you all I know is all I have
To trade or live by
No daily corner calls me at daybreak
But somehow I must live:

I don't know what I will shout in your streets

THE MARKS ARE WAITING

Our new acuity
Has been misread
As short attention span
But all our aptitude for euphemism
Has been stretched
Like the elastic
In a pair of drawers
Floating around our hips
Uncomfortably
We behold the birth of a new world
Odder than the ones before
In the blue gloom of TV light in Darien
In Pueblo Heights, in College Station
Imagination waiting
Our shopping malls explode with petrojunk
Become necessities
Recycled endlessly
As yellow ribbon

The computers spit out
Inventories of foreshortened amnesia
Long lists of metaphors now obsolete
Willing acceptance of the reprehensible
Lite War
Reports of suffering
Enough to satisfy
But low on passion

You must give up outmoded ideas
New and improved
Marinetti to Super Mario III
Forget
Honor or hygiene
Flushing the planet with
Blood

It's cleaner to think of
Punitive surgery
Competition
Forget it   old hat
Sort of like a lethal Olympics
Strategy   A game of checks
A commerce cruel enough to make E. F. Hutton
Hard sell canard
Shut up but not shut down
Patriotism or the ploy du jour?
The boys in the backroom
Will come up with an ideology
If that still gets it

A 24–7 sideshow
No business but police business
It's never out it's never over
Is what remains, a bit of theater
Going on all the time
A murderous roadshow
With out-of-town tryouts
For smart bombs and stealth politicians
Without a Broadway to go to

■

If history can still be understood as a record of the deeds of leaders, then the recent history of the United States is the record of bizarre plots and frantic attempts to cover their behinds performed by an amazingly conscienceless batch of born-again hypocrites and felons-in-waiting. Shameless and possibly insane, these men have presided over the decay of both cities and countryside and the demoralization of citizens facing a plummeting standard of living.

If history is properly a narrative of the collective tropism of masses of people, then our recent history is the tale of a populace mesmerized by ever more technically elaborate and intellectually vacuous entertainments designed to distract them from their deepening poverty.

All of the traditional events of the Olympic games are, in fact, martial arts. The rationale of the games, however, is the display of martial prowess in the interest of intertribal nonbelligerence. If these "war games" can, in fact, be construed as simultaneous competition and international cooperation, we have a perfect model for conceptual confusion that can do much more than merely stimulate sales of beer, exercise clothing, and motor vehicles.

For a population addicted to entertainment, demented leaders have invented real war presented as games. The names should be familiar: Grenada, Panama, Kuwait (or Iraq). There are also the minor league games: El Salvador, Nicaragua. Then there's the really funky training camp called Bosnia. Somehow, if you ask folks, you'll find that most people know more details about the 1956 World Series than about any of these campaigns. But each one was presented in the papers and on the radio and TV just like the real thing and—of course—for the unfortunate human beings maimed or killed in those places, it *was* the real thing.

In *Nineteen Eighty-Four*, George Orwell showed how leaders could manipulate populations by preying upon a usefully inarticulate combination of patriotism and self-interest. Ray Bradbury's *Fahrenheit 451* went further in showing the way that scapegoating becomes the instrumentality of such a system. The current permanent crisis provides opportunity for ambitious men to keep busy while thinking they are performing historic deeds; and the public, fitfully distracted by incomprehensible events occurring in never-heard-of places, remains confused. Gore Vidal, educated to find causes for effects, has guessed that the transformation of the United States into a "national security state" in the late 1940s explains the subsequent armed adventures of the past decade, but that means taking these escapades seriously. Actually, the old Roman recipe for ruling is at work: keep the people in line with bread and circuses.

Less bread, more circuses. When there's really nothing worth seeing, the show goes on all night long.

DIRGE FOR AMADOU DIALLO

It is hard to have your son die
In a distant land

If they said he was a soldier
We would pray
The way we always pray
That his would be the *final* sacrifice
And we would understand

Questions will fill
That churning emptiness
Shaped like a boy
Grown beautifully into a man
There'll be no answers
Still, we'll understand

If he was a true believer
Or a missionary
Apostle or a revolutionary
Ardent altruist or visionary
—in these mean times?
Maybe instead
A hard and nerveless man,
A mercenary
Then we would dread
His noble loss or petty glory
And we would understand

It is hard to have your son die
In a distant land

If accident
Or heart attack
We could blame chance
Or curse our earthbound ignorance

        Vow to concoct new mythologies
That wouldn't
Forge us such raw cruelties
Marching our hope
In coffles toward the grave

We'd understand
If someone said he was,
This son, a prodigal:

        The kind of man who desperately
Needs the vise of suffering
And hurt and desolation
Some eccentricity to hold him firm
To help him shape his heart
Into an instrument of praise

        The kind of man
Who dares to summon whirlwinds
To winnow wisdom from sophistication
        O we would wail
And hold our heads
Astonished by the wastefulness of Fate
        This repetitious wastefulness of Fate
And understand

But now they tell me
Of a peaceful man
A mother's son, a father's pride
        Seeking to study
In the learned halls
Of a distant, splendid,
Powerful, affluent land
        A young man murdered murdered
And murdered at the hand
Of men sworn to uphold the Law
Not thugs or bandits
        And there's no justice?
There's no recompense?

O no,
In spite of all our history of terror
In the world
Uncountable eons of sorrow
Of the world
O no, O no
We do not understand

It is hard to have your son die
In a distant land
And harder still
When we can't understand

AN AFTERNOON WITH DR. BLUMENBACH

... yet in the beauty of our Saviour blacknesse is commended,
When it is said, his locks are bushie and black as a Raven.
—Sir Thomas Browne

Light with a veil of dust
Climbs through the window
And pauses to investigate
A shelf of skulls

This new disguise suits me
I think. To probe
To not disturb the Doctor's thoughts
Though I intrude

Methodical and passionless
The Doctor places shot into the scales
Weighing a fragile monument
To breath and sadness

His concentration like a steady flame
Would please Hermes
Bent to a greater task
Than Adam's charge from God
Man to name Man himself
To rank and classify his tribes

The Doctor's sure science
Cannot predict advent of fools
Alfalfa Bill in academic robes
Like Nott and Stoddard

Doctors with heads as empty
As those on his shelf
And hearts as cold as bone

Calling accursed
My own beloved ones
Who dance my tropics
Praising me
Into whose faces
I have signed my name

But in this one I'll invest some time

Of course, my visit cannot take too long
I have more calls to make
A fierce Red poet waits
And then a young American
On Fire Island

I wonder should I beg him to come ride with me
And make a housecall on a troubled century

Crowded with those who cannot even see
The universal skull beneath the skin

Doctor, what must we do
To make them see the light within?

V

Dangerous Doubts

DANGEROUS DOUBTS

The mind invents its own inadequacies
But not the power to erase illusion
That schemes and wholesome dreams
Can become actual despite the truth
That thoughts invest themselves in flesh
And direct motion

That you have 30,000 shots at immortality
But only one you dare not miss at being rich
Or at the least escape the nag of destitution

That maybe exercise shows on TV
Are really harmful
That sound bodies just
Amplify our empty minds

That platitudes contain a grain of wisdom

And fortune's a rush hour train that doesn't wait

To really live means needing other people
That whatever that means love
Could conquer hate

LUSTRE

What does the warmth
Of your hand mean
That accompanies
The mute slide into sleep
When she feels like a shoemaker's children
All your endearments spent
On lavish wit
Or lyrics mailed away

Trading compliments feels
Like having dinner with strangers
Conversation predicted
The weather, a sadness shared
About the world today
(Art) (land) (livestock) auction prices
The polished surface of civility

Is this warmth ardor or a vital sign?
Bad married love or good
Clairvoyance
Your hand   your heart
The hot comb in the radio
That pulled Glenn Miller's Orchestra
Out of the sky

CAMEO IN SUDDEN LIGHT

How possibly could I
Fall in love with you
From looking at the back of your
Head
The care of studious hands
Shadowed curls
One broken sequin
Glittering and hiding
On gray carpeted step
Rustle of an intruding word
In a sea of paper, full of words
Fading and slowly writhing
Like traders of fable
In a haunted green quadrant
Carefully natural and tended
Tourista allure
A 2-foot stack of powdering disasters,
Yellow pathos, wrinkled household
Hints
Frayed recipes and task force reports
Of one dowdy crisis after another
Discovered the deed
Costing into the thousands
As the shy light of a lost sequin
Blurts into fuchsia anxiety
No, I don't want you to see me

We are stealing avalanches of light
These several things
Seeking glimmers of focus
Each in our part of the room
Hiding and shining
Kuji Kiri the Ninja technique
Of performing hypnotic hand movements
Sha   the 5th center of power

Opening the Eight Psychic Channels
Begins at the base of the balls
Flows to the solar plexus
Tu Mo the base of the spine
Jen Mo at home in your brain
The body is one ocean
After another, secret and blue
Holding treasures when you have mastered
This motion

Much is promised
Power
Is useful only when
She hides her face
Within the shadow of a jeweled hand
When she beckons
A mystic light in Bermudian waters
A potted tree that forces you
To cross gleaming lobbies
To prove that the blossoms are silk
And abject poverty and ingenuity
And love of beauty
Will steer our troubled course
As long as there are sad-faced maidens
Bending and shaping flowers in Taiwan
We are bright and alive in our security
Gasping as if rocketing upward
Out of travel brochure blue
Is not of the much that is promised

Amusing wall shadows are included
Attract popular and becoming friends!
High side those who once snubbed you!
Strange and colorful phonecalls
Will come to you from unpronounceable places!
But power is one thing you won't get

How could I
Possibly
Go on this way
Without you
At least sending some
Some discreetly placed
Signal
Seal it
With the voice of a seashell
The whorl of a conch
Or gleam of ancilla
Salvager,
For God's sake
Turn around

COUNTRY SONG

Don't know a thing
Except what I know:
I like great big legs
& where they go

I love the colors in the Arkansas sky
When the sun goes down
And I'm as lonely as an empty chair
When you're not around

MULTICULTURAL

Watch who ends up in contestant's row
I like it when the colored people win
It always was all women years ago
Once in a while maybe a young Marine
LCpl in dress uniform
Every other word he said was "sir"
Probably a newlywed on top of that
You know he's going to win a car
Or bedroom suit
Not that the game is fixed but to be fair
I'm sure someone at CBS
Made lots of money figuring this out
Before I did
The way they've got it now
All kinds of people get to come on down
OK by me. But yet and still
I like it when the colored people win

LOW RIDER

Kind of guy
who wants 3 kids
Loves being "Popi!"
May be a reluctant groom
like most sane men

An ideal husband
if she understands
His wildness and dictatorship
And all his pride
except her & the kids

Is dancing in that loud garage
& all those intense hours
Making his lime-green Malibu
Trace perfectly the daft *dressage*
Of a distracted Colonel's
Most haughty palomino

For more
How to Keep Peace in Your Home

See our
next installment

AN EVEN-TEMPERED GIRL HOLDS HER BREATH

He looked for mischief
But he only found
Tantrums so slight
They wouldn't register
On any instrument
Less finely gauged
Than she in time
Tuned him to be

Um hmm

She holds her breath
A beat

If he forget me, I could disappear
Like this

Silently fading and slowly
Like an ancient VistaVision movie

Shown very late at night
So ineptly lensed
The only evidence of lovers seen
One nose and one nose
On each edge of the TV screen
As they are heard
Talking, dramatically pledging

Or better yet, *he* could

mmmm Huhnh!

SHE LIVED TO BE 100

Oriki for William A. Thomas, His Goodness and Strength

The first person I ever knew
who died
The last I can recall
to exit dreaming
The whole house knew
something was wrong
That morning
Broad daylight stood
in every window
Boldly shining
And he was still
in bed in his pajamas

A KIND OF ACCOUNTING

Habana and the pretty ocean
Then Miami
Each stop a little less Spanish
And then LaGuardia

My Uncle Robert large and handsome
As the sun itself on the tarmac
Resplendent in a pinstripe suit
And camel benny
Shrugged on his shoulders Russian Jewish style
Huge enough to fling bold toreador
Around my dad's whole little family

Expansive gesture

But he wouldn't lend his brother money
And ridiculed his job
When he finally found one

He said "I didn't get what I got
Through bad investments"
Then made a half a dozen
Right away as years went by

But every New Year's Eve
Always at Robert's lavish Harlem party
Warmed
Full of greens black-eyed peas VO and Redd Foxx records
The brothers compared notes
Laughing & fully armed with wary candor
Watching each other prosper in New York

CUTE GIRL WITH A TOY MONKEY

Looks like the girl I loved
When I was young
Whose name   whose name
        is on the tip of my tongue
But it doesn't matter

She was the generic one
The one that was perfect
For me

Does she look like an angel?
No. She looks like a girl

Rapt in calm concentration
Peacefully. Transported on thought

I can't imagine her being loud
Well, except under certain circumstances

Her sparkling eye light
And pursed lips
She's either very happy with herself
Or nuts

So beautiful!

I change for the F train at Roosevelt
And watch her
        gliding away
But at 71st and Continental
Here she is again!
        boarding my train

That girl that is perfect for me
That I never got

When I looked for Beatrice
I found you

When I looked for Eurydice
I found you

When I wasn't looking for anybody at all
I found you

That's what, Fate?

FLASH POINT

This useless clairvoyance
Is embarrassing
What good is it to know
The motives behind manners

And worse, the so what stares
Of those upon whom you manage
To inflict this wisdom

There is more space
Awaiting exploration
More clouds of gas
That need their picture took

GOD SENDS LOVE DISGUISED AS ORDINARY PEOPLE

We never quite could tell
strength from stupidity
Pride in perseverance
The point where stubbornness
Purchased a harvest of futility

If the body has forgotten how to sleep
what chance has thought
To teach it subtleties
Like tenderness or faith

All that could matter
is the reciprocating warmth
Of flesh—wordless and beyond translation
to idea or category
Nothing numerical and yet
Not boundless, either
Nothing so grand or abstract

In other words,
we were not brutes for lack of feeling
Nor sorrowful in spiteful isolation
Not lonely yet
But damaged by avoiding touch
Being only smart enough to trust
That there's some
gifted outcast family
Somewhere a troop of *djalis*
That still performs the music that we need
To reconnect our feet to dirt
To fling our arms like windmills
Spinning in dusted twilight

The point being not that you beat
yourself up appreciating
That so and so has done for you
But that you finally remember
You've been her gypsy, too

MAGNETIC CHARMS

I'm saying
I have outgrown promises
Not you

Call it
Reality because there is
no better word

To call our secrets
Falsity that haunts us
With the fear
That what we know and hide
Is all we are

But if false actions
haunt us
What faith
Old women in small villages
in backward lands
Could possibly find resonance
In words?

When I touch you
That zone of heat
Beneath my hand—
Trust that

What do you call
a trouble shared
Check "strength" or "weakness"
The cancer patients
smoking on the patio, for instance

Incorrigibles
Roaring, indignant, daring the world's end
With love of laughter
As if to say
"We lived and live our lives
                                        this way
And won't regret it
                                even when we change"

I do not think that I can
Guarantee the truth
By plan or force of will

And fear that disappointing you
        will undo me
Not you

What I have given in majestic arrogance or quiet need
Does it glow in you?

Does it calm or warm
Or furnish afternoons with peaceful hours?

I am the one I do not wish
        to leave bereft
Not you

I'm saying

The last time I walked on Lake Conroe
It kind of gave way

EQUINOX

It was an act of stealth
And troubled pleasure
—Wordsworth, The Prelude *(1850)*

I

There may be other roles you recognize
        Sailors at nightwatch
Soldiers on picket

But we are shepherds now
And it is Spring!

And we are talking …

OK, so we're not shepherds
But this is useful play

Like shepherds on a dark hillside
Drawing lines between the stars,
        We reach beyond ourselves
To meet ourselves

Or are we talking
Just to fill the space between us
        To get over
A century that ends
        in fireworks
And worldwide efforts
To undo the future?

Then we were dancing …

This is my real life.
The day is still wet
        from morning's rain
Pavements begin to steam

Killer 1970s guitars
        rattling the dash
Driving west into a majolica landscape
the city in the rearview
        clasped by night
Abandoned by the sun

At best, a graveyard chance
        "Time to get your grip
& move on ..."

¡O preach us some pleasant nonsense,
        Por favor!

Amuse us, O Lord!
        We are the audience
For your sneak preview
        of heaven!

Thrust into this florid maze,
Trust curiosity
To find its way
To cleverness
A long-awaited legion of idolaters
Arriving after giddy pilgrimage

        Then came the prismed vision
As we saw the world through tears

II

No, it is Spring!

Three days of rain,
        not Biblical
But more than this ground
Could take

Standing water everywhere

After 3 days of rain
They look like lakes
These fields near Hockley
        fields waiting for cotton
Corn or say
Tract homes or condominiums
        Or little malls
Glimmering like fish-scales in the sun
As a sheet of egrets settles in
        beside the lakes
That will not be here
        in three days
In fields that will not be here
        in three years

        But we were talking …

Shepherds,
Or boys at useful play

You find the married men at 4 o'clock
Leaning against their trucks
        beside the road
Sharing half-pints or 6-packs
Or, in the city, at a cocktail lounge
Trying to prolong the day's escape

But there are others
        who are not here
Men
Who have years to speak of
Farmers, retired mechanics

Old men gather at breakfast
To direct the day into its starting gate
Booting the sun along a slotted course
Above the never-ending shadow puppet dance of power
The energetic pettiness of mundane business

These high priests of expected disappointments
Raise their polyphonic song:
Life is unpleasant   but predictable

If this is solace,
These men standing
    up against the wall
These are the guardians
Of future pathways—

    But it is Spring!

III

You feel like skipping
But the costume
Wants a more processional step

Will there be ruins where we walk?
Will our footfalls echo purposes?

Count this, if not as blessing
Then as a good thing:

Talking together as gray-haired men
    with the guy
You looked up at the stars with
When you were boys

And wondering if there's a God
    a girl, a goal
A meaning to the universe
& knowing now
    you really do not know much more
Than you did back then,

These conversations
Like a diamond's facets
Like sunlight on fields suddenly make lakes
The subject always the same
Yet seems transparently
Deflecting something deeper
More personal—demanding
More attention
When you think it over
As you will, inventing
What you should have said
Too late for that now
And next time will be deceiving

A boy's job
To listen to the old men's lies
And learn the music—

> *A boy's job is*
> *To listen to the old men lie*
> *& learn the music . . .*

I never been nowhere
Where the old Blues singers been

But I swear to my soul
I don't want to go there again

BACK-ORDERED TEARS

It was when neon was no longer available
That they went mad.
There was nothing to cut the Formica.
Offbeat shouting dirty words
Dropping glitter on backward lands
Nothing seemed to help.

It was quarter to 2 in a small, dull town
Jukebox exhausted, coffee burned stale
A go-go girl sluffs on her bedroom slippers
Punches some feeling back into her thighs.

It was in those days musicians started dancing
Didn't have to touch their instruments.
In fact, they couldn't even stop the music playing
It was so much sadness in the world.

Additional Poems

THE BLACK CANARIES WEEP OVER GOMORRHA

eating your petals in the afternoon
will rot

                    my teeth
                    & guts on rainy nights

& when we chew the petals
of each other's
tongue

the rot is sure
to spread & that's
too bad

because your mouth really
is a fine place for
geraniums &c.

carousing
in some
cold but
sunny street
I find yr
name dangling
on a string between
me legs

: flower name
for dryrot
girl / strange spaces

b
r
e
a
k

our
lips
& split
my words

SOUTH AFRIKA

(when the white cold marble
turns gray and the columns

of the palace crumble with
roars of gladness) there will

be no escaping the nature
of the bitter flesh.

when the rockdrill
pounds away beneath the earth

beating its *hard bon*
into the summer twilight

the loam will yellow
and the palace will fall.

and the blue, blue
lights of sorrow that swing

in well-worn arcs above
the balustrados will be

ten million flickering torches.
There'll be white-clear freedom

(the red wind won't blow)
for old black joe.

A TALE OF TWO CITIES

"They were like wild animals," said M. Djoumessi
—New York Times, *25 February 1960*

O the wild dancers, the New York
beer-drinkers, running amok at the UN shouting,
"You've crucified our saintly Lumumba . . ."

And what about the people's other saints
In Bklyn, do storefront churches worship
a storefront God?
And elsewhere are there rites? Rights, riots?
How does the mask fit elsewhere on this fraud
that we call life?
The Times says nights in Cameroun are terrible.
Young intellects, old madmen, philosophers and
poets, machete the non-believers of their
political voudoun.
Who are their saints, what are their rituals?
Who sings their hymns, Geo. Beverly Shay or
Clara Ward or good ol' Charlie Mingus?

My friend, their ritual is death and their
hymns are marching songs and the groans of their
victims.
Gen. Moumie gange cinq million Soldat. Yaounde,
Bassa, Grassfield!

The screams of victims. Mr. Mingus.
Yaounde, yaounde, yaounde.

GRASS

Some evil eye bewitches my lambkins.
—Vergil, Eclogues *III, 113*

I

Sang the flaying of trees, black-flecked gold in sixty-foot current,
he did.
Oh, but the voice of that wind, the long droning, and pages
of Keats in a book she'd had to bring for both of them, somehow fell flat
against the walled and closeted lust (drooping flower worn lapelled and
pinned).
And he, embarrassed in another song, tracing
the Cessna's path above the trees, knowing Keats's caelus in his sky,
that Keats would visit him at midnight, saying: "Eyes on the mottled sky,
watching
for aircraft yet! It's ocean reflects all passions of the
heart, enfolds, and rings all changes." Some think it's grass.
Under the trees and behind them, there're children carousing through
lunch-times. There's traffic you can hear and even see,
lift yourself to the chair arm, eyelevel above the peeling sill.
Ignore the flaking paint. Insides of things, easychairs, have a story;
a world that's now gone under the sea.

II

Gardening! How else to get your hands down in the clay and still be
civilized,
be non-subversive? Gardening, yes. A way to get inside the furniture.
There's a primal world beneath the springs
of any couch, a jungle in box-springs, a midwest inside every mattress!
Listen, you know nothing of nature. Nor difference between excelsior
and wheat.
You'd call this nature, your crazy green grove on a hill?
That grove's grass is even forbidden, someone else's urban turf.
Ah no, give me furniture that's quiet, fat about the waist, a little out
of it and

Don't talk to me of gardening in real soil: that summer, backyard
perversion. It doesn't make it. It's three generations, I think, fill
the house across the street and everyone of 'em
stooped, proud, wearing gray hair. Backyard gardeners all,
a housefull of perverts. The second son (he's gray-haired like the rest)
leans in the heat with electric saw, two axes and, blood rising in narrow,
naked chest, works over some determined stump. That's far from Christian
behavior.
An old man at that, his gray hair the mark of his sin.

And what does sitting on the grass mean anyway? What magick,
what pacific whisperings rise from the morning jewels of its hair?
No fold-up loveseat pales
before the long wind-harrowed field.

III

Seeing young girls flopped on the summer benches or lying on the campus
green at noon, light cotton dresses tucked in around their knees, is
everything that nature means to me. Oh, if I could have that rustic
furniture
and kooky Alcippe to sprawl there with, without a cop to whistle down
the gathered crowd: satyrs and naiads, with Damoetas humming verses
to his pope and no salaried spoilsport in the area, I'd forget the shade
of chrome interiors, forget the suggestive symmetry
of dining tables and my passion for upholstered furnishings.

IV

They smirk at me. Who'd once eat up my jive now laugh when I sit in
the shade,
flute 'cross my lap. The bucolic's out of style? Why blame
Menalcas, his Arcadia's only twenty acres wide and hardly wooded. Like
a jackrabbit bounding up the steps to a library or a lazy tabby adopted
by custodians and bright young girls, Menalcas stays embarrassed in the
golden season. Fault's not his grasp of pastoral form uh unh the char-

acters that fill his vale. "The trouble with 'em," he says, "they're so
goddam in bloom. No dear departed shepherd boy for miles around and yet
I had to sing. Aw, look at 'em, longing for the grass."
And he and I, excelsior pushing through our just-framed springs,
retire to an old room in the house for the removal of a certain snood.

WEST

Hot afternoons have been in Montana
—Eli Siegel

Randolph Scott sweat X-ing his back his yellow shirt too
a tau on spine and shoulders. Hard man he is and grizzled living a
lonely time in an open country color of rust.
Ho where the rock rises straight as a dropped plumb.
Ho colour of rust rising yes from spare grasslands.
Buttes what they call 'em. Hard they calls themselves.
Also the soft fellow in the B' way movie think they're hard men do they?
They know Scott's got him a lollipop in his smelly pocket? Fifteen
worn greenbacks in his unwashed levis?
No breeze on the silvered plains only soft blasts   soft blasts   in the
big Fedders behind the baroque wall. And the balcony roof leaking
goddamit. And the bitch at the popcorn forty two a redhead
much too heavy and nasty personality too.
So how come Scott's widow-woman's blond & twenty six doesn't even
wear a bra never mind girdle? So how come the sailors in their whites
try to slide along the tapestry when they float in? They cruisers?
Hmmm and then everybody's thinking about Randolph
only me about the widow's bra.

Now could I read Browning.
"Home
Thoughts from abroad
& it still lucid, cool streams descend
for every corpulent jew.

My fingers" (accentuated
my eyes heavy-lidded
and my fingers thick. They magazine

silver to christianize
my palm.
This is a set of affairs
like warm adventures in darkest africa "Afric-ay"

Ah, forty years ago.

entire geography history a jumbled a yellow in fireside
pages my yellow, O something tender about
the ending
lines the feminine poem
"There will always be a place for you
you can be the epee
when I paint the heart on my chest

ENURESIS

The white sails thicken out on the bay
I am watching the girls on the street they run down into subways
Julia bends into the breeze,
I am watching the boats bank and heading for port
The water churns in the wind. Now the clouds drop a dank haze
Over the water. Everything makes me think of the afternoon's cold
    glass
Filling with ron rico. I am watching the portugese girls on the
    pier, the yellow
Oilskins. I am pulling my quiet rubber hood on against the rain.
Yesterday I came late and you were angry. Remember the last
Time you got so angry, it isn't good for my health. My worn nerves,
    anything short
Of idylls depresses me. Rum depresses me, everything makes me think
    of boats.
The American plan depresses me. They will send me to seattle for
    ninety-seven years
To pay off our trip to Habana. Was it worth it, I lost my whole
    paycheck
In the casino. I am listening to the slow music of the cables, the
    boats are lost.
Slow music depresses me. The Coast Guard depresses me. The alarums
    of the south
Shore, the birds they always bring along with them.
I am looking at all the pretty girls in their portugese foul weather
    coats
Everything is so green. Foul weather depresses me. Your house makes
    my mouth
Sticky with whispering my voice is pitched too low for whispering.
I am watching the name Cleopatra in egyptian hieroglyphics, gray
    birds over the neck
Of the bay. I am watching the islands in the bay, the graves of
    birds murdered last
Summer by United Airlines. Businessmen depress me. I am all alone
    in the boat

Watching the shore pull me home. I am poverty-struck where's the
        pawnshop, I hock
All my clothes for a dollar. We are on the subway, I am watching
        two pr punks
Terrorize everybody. Look, they are kicking that old woman in her
        damn head. Terror
Depresses me
The air falls on the city in great cold chunks and the glistening
        tide covers
All of south queens. From the highway the lights attack the city
        and freeze
The people in their little houses. LaGuardia chills them on the
        Sound, is the north
Shore even colder than the weather near Jamaica Bay they seem to
        think so in Flushing.
You are putting your hand in my glove. Stop it, the Coast Guard
        is watching.
There are analogies about houses we learn them in winter. I am
        polishing the greaves
Of Class 3A sailboats. They are splintery and thin. Their owners
        starve them.
I am thinking of dogs more valuable than all of us, they strain
        against electrified
Fences at the secret laboratory as she feeds them their medicinal
        slop
I am thinking about black and white pictures (halftones) and
        nautical children.
I am thinking of General Douglas MacArthur. Starvation depresses
        me. I just thought
Of big gray snow clouds. Like 4th of July bunting

GILBERT AND SULLIVAN

Here is no redly opulent Cossack no painted Trinity
Church flat, no warm emergent April.
Here is autumn matins, the love of natural seasons, thermal
Underwear
Frustrated butterflys they aren't leaves
But poorly typed pages
Here is a difficult island, be very
Careful which of the wild and sometimes gaudy fruit you may eat here.
A darkly beautiful girl will impersonate Penelope
Here, with fondly erratic ingenues
Othello enjoys his greasepaint troubles & they the midnight pleasures he gives.
The leading lady's a bitch she slurs all the witty phrases
As troublesome as any woman be,
There's always some girl at The Actor's Studio who'll work after some coaching. See
Now the people come onstage in decorous twos

ANOTHER ABSTRACT ETC

He said, "Why must it also smite; the hand that feeds
O my little garden
you are to me vineyard field meadow and wood

He spread out a brief on the table,
together with a sort of
diagram. "She said she was afraid," said John doggedly.

"What can I do about it now? Throw myself on old Numidian lovers
only to be scorned by their insulted husbands ..."
Suddenly he turned on Hauser. "Hauser, I could kill you!"
John grimaced and wrung his hands,

wild, greening trees and shadows filled the place
O god! to have to choose between two women and there's no way to
have both.
"Then I must shoot myself." The water rushed out of his ear!

THE CONSCIENCE OF COLE PORTER

OK so a piece of his head is intact
The part with the row of dots crossing the forehead
Whee! Now we are going straight down his flat
Nose between the eyes.
You are wondering why I asked you to come here this evening. The
        bed
Is rumpled, the hard stare breed the tome a gloom
Do you think we'll ever understand it
Awkward vessels, "bathing in onion and Worcestershire"
O it is so scary the "milleflor"
        the Cloisters
The same feeling that we have been
What ingeniously begins as a sonnet, unscrupulously an exercise
        in mystery form
Nodding "nodding" both intuitive and the demanded word,
You are miraculous even outside your own
Here, moving deep into the garden so many times before.
Conception, and it
Barely pleases you. Then he a stone Shadow, you are so far gone

(Lamont Cranston)

THE PORNOGRAPHY

The desk is brown where Milan sits,
emphatic days correct
these long clean sheets where he has collected
women for his papers. Now my hand rests
longingly on the keys
Yesterday I was no slave to such fake acrostic brilliance
My hand stuck in her groin, she whispers
“This is 5th Avenue, stupid. Please
behave yourself until later.”
And later it rained so heavily that the sink in the kitchen
backed up. I know it has something to do with
natural science. She dresses me tonight as her alchemist
and my green starry robes
fly like hounded birds gee whiz I am a prophet exalted in the wind.
“People, imagine what it is like to make love in an airplane
What are all these blue things,” she says
as we leave the quiet red barn.
There’s no God and there’s no Buddha, said Gautama. This is not me.

LINEAR VARIATION

for Ted Greenwald

I

Here is a sentence. "A rose and a vase are there"
I am writing this poem on the run, I don't even stop to breathe
Hardly. Inheritors of a common tradition,
Teeth set on edge. This book is to carry with one by the waters. O see the miles
In his grey sweats come up the weed path. His smelly ease
Is his perversion and it pants for him. He's come so far that his strong
Legs may buckle so he can sleep in Africas dreary
As when a man named Rhodes from Baltimore faces the ruins of a village.
It is this melancholy thing, this deviation without possibility
Notice them now as you go along.

II

Here is another sentence, this one is truer:
This is a damn presumptuous thing for me to be saying. Don't knock
It though just on the baldness of it, think of a whole
Line of blue shirted track stars they sweat in the eternal Roman sun,
All of them running for the United States. Or, in another way.
I love a woman that I myself created, she gleans
The ripe ears of my celibacy and the laws of 40 states prevent our marriage.
The landscape's thoroughly tropic where she meets
Me, ablaze with capes & crocks,
Angora sweaters. Maybe this old greek mama in the quaking subway
Could let me know the lineage of cranes,
She with the handbag full of Aegean fruit who ignores the public and simply eats.

NICHOMACHEAN ETHICS

Humph, we French negroes wrest fantastic music from our radiant lunch
Camembert cheese and gingery romaine, and in the fields
Sow barley where it will never grow perhaps a greeny follicle
May deliver hair, hair that will grow magnificently strong impaling heroes
Their drooling beast animals that dance in my chest

Come, rest in my deep hairy Abraham's bosom I'll be the father
You can depend on me if you're ever at loose ends if they repossess your furniture
Come home to my curly white beard you have a rain house in my rib
Could be easier could it to talk about things, animals deep in my chest
In some driftwood Marcel Duchamp blues I lost my baby, I almost lost my mind
Friday I make pilgrimages to my sweet momma's room to look at familiar
Pictures all the pretty rose wallpaper there.

CHORUS FROM AN UNWRITTEN GREEK PLAY

(WOODWINDS)

vision of the pastoral, the green
weeds at the lonely vicarage or by
the back door in the heat of fox trot dance
hall, don't knock it jim, you wouldn't
rather have a palladium for spics
living under a weird tradition
of Europe's stifling conceit, Toynbee
thinking I will save the whore
of dying Europe with my savagery and
blanching when I ask him why I should.

(LAMENT, BARITONE)

all of this complete wasted on me.
the lines of vision broken,
cracked like biscuits on the rocks.
smoke rises, holocaust, columns.

THE COLOR SECTION

"Here, you see the weird lives of the Amish
Typical in every way, disguised in the
Expanse of the brown lawn" Or maybe an
Old fisherman's collection of plaster sharks,
Statuettes of Davy Jones and beer bottles
Found by young girls on some european beach
Color photos of all the nearby junior colleges,
A beautiful starlet on the cover.
Deeper into the fuzzy print, lumpy animals stray
Across the empty hand of the main house
Because Sunday afternoon has arrived at last.
Once or twice the hands turned a page
When the treatments began, white and heavy
People drive up to the windows, park and
Come into the house They don't make
Me lose any high at all (even at the same time my body
Does and much more quick, too. Restlessness
Pumps up my legs again   )
It is partly the way somebody comes up with a shovel
And buries an important object in his garden.
Over my head is a corner of the yellow kitchen, a
Plastic bag in front of my face. I am not wearing my glasses
And   reaching for them   they flop and
Flutter joyously in my hand. Like some unusual bird,
I can even feel the bone crumbling in my jaw
Just like looking up into a blue sky that means "day"
My cigarettes start to taste like shit and
It's a new brand, too. I just want to turn on again,
Pick up a western Berlin color section etc
With an article on jazz and none of these corny features.
I don't want to think about any more lynchings
Here, you see the foundering lives of die schwartze
Then music that makes horrible pleasures, drugs.
The kitsch space of a common, empty New York City sky
Brown arms out of my t shirt, and the new Remington II.

Islands capped with imitation spanish red-roof
Stucco houses   that is the only thing I understand
About Florida   Thousands of red Impala convertibles floating
Into the city along the white causeway. And
On the colored ferry line I discover the 4th of July
Further down the coast, a magazine all about power boating
A theory, how shrivelled and useless clean houses

THE JUDGMENT OF PARIS

Come on with the foliage! Paris may make
An error in judgment, any blankets
For Paris and "the victorious one"
To go to bed inside of? Or underneath—

In each case Paris is covered with feathers.
Paris like an accountant discovered at
The racetrack Saratoga "for health pur-
Poses" Not the hawk feathers of Ghengis Khanh

The co-workers gather around their water-
Cooler to talk about Paris. Paris bobs
Upright in the cooler, and the cups
On the wall are marked "German High Command"

Paris has $16,000,000 in the little black
Schoolbag. The truth would just "black-
Up" the feathers covering Paris, it's time to make
Up some good lies

THE FALL OF PARIS

Paris is dead. The citizens of Paris again
Ruin the streets with their placards
Oui! now that the black 38 Packard
Comes around the corner   the gun muzzle

Out of the window. Now that our Paris
Has been murdered on the street, the
Citizens demand satisfaction   What mob
Sent over the blasters of Paris?

Paris looks down from the highest gate
In the city. There is a blinding
Flash and then Paris tumbles to
The ground, like an island floating

Out of the continental mass called "The Sky"
Mon dieu! Afternoons are so terrible
It's October in Paris and new revolutions
Like compost on every side of town.

ROBERT WILLIAMS, EXILED IN CUBA

Say Que pasa to Nicolás Guillén, Wilfredo Lam.
Tell them I say hello. Look in the streets
for a dark boy, look where the students hang out, a dark boy
with three strong hairs on his dry chin,
find him and say, "Lorenzo's
in New York this winter and, you know, he's black too.

Lorenzo, born in Panama, could look from
his playpen, see the Canal Zone, the stars & stripes.
Could see Uncle Sam's guns aimed at the nazi.
Lorenzo, flying to the states in '47,
Stopped over in Havana one hour, remembers little."

It's snowing. People pass me on the street
in their long, flashy coats. Sheep-skin,
green loden, shades of brown, black, dark loam.
My knowledge of distances, these colors burn and crunch against each other,
measurements crumple. Hands jammed into big pockets,
fleece maws they follow
the dog-chain breath & their warm, thick-pile coats cradle
unenvied burdens: dust, washable dyes, traces
of hamburger served on day-old buns.

They say to me, "It's not so bad up here.
You bitch too much. New York City, this enlightened,
liberal year! My coat is even black,
it's not North Carolina."
Hey Williams, Edgar Hoover's got no price on me.
But someone has. Nobody held my granny in the kitchen,
but I speak inglés with a Harlem tint
and that's not advantage, man. Do I need to talk
about the way they crush me, walking the street in their long coats?
Williams, find that boy. Tell him in spanish: Lorenzo's
in New York, it's snowing. He sits in a warm room,
going blind.

SONNET

The birds around here are terrible.
They've beat the trees to death
and stabbed the deafening campanile
in the back. Red insects bite the flowers
in the neck and open-mouthed WW 1
aeroplanes skywrite obscenities on
the bell tower's stained glass

head, (isn't it something? I don't
mind when you call me two-faced because
when the train doors open up, the
fresh air blowing between my faces
feels so nice) The wounded campanile
has spoken. Early in the morning
its white heart rings like broken glass.

LIFE ON THE FARM

for Don Newcombe

That year they really wanted a negro fireman.
Alone on the north forty
I studied the Arco manuals, pages flipping the slight
Wind blowing from Montreal my heart a slight
Easterly flutter.
Cultural exchange farmers came from Russia to visit and I paused
To polish the tractors. Later, I studied
In town. That same winter I studied
The seasons. I'll never look at that first year over my shoulder
Every time I said, "Now can I go to the mound"
A typical obsession with rookies. The mound
Over 30 yards through the outfield
Animal worship was all the rage that year, returning me to Denver
Here, where you find me "planted in Denver"

PROJECT BLUES

The revolutions are half of the postcard
Secretly in his shoe to remind him of America
And the noxious dialectics of her wealthy
Peasants, who stand around in sequined rags
Knocking on the black doors of soft evil
That have escaped the Evil committees and
After tea (huh) the solarium makes it impossible
To continue his mushmouth lower-class habit
The overhauls walk in the room like a man
Visits our dilapidated yearning with devices
Of an exhausted white haired politician we
Come to depend on and trust in spite of
Inclement weather teasing our picnics at
Cpl Dennison Park blue sky bends the trees
To its will The animals gaze on us from
Back the flowered park as we eat barbecue
Dance to impractical music and speeches
Poof! The following day another imposter
Who freshens his kerchief with brine and go party
Surrounds himself with nebulous seasons
From which his pretty lies are detracted
Drowning the parquet of unbelievable flowers
His ship comes over the acid spew and horizon
As the discard of innocuous self-indulgence
Where she waits in her red wig although he is
The culprit hearing these sentences bind him
She will not have him even for the gigolo price
It says on the wall of his heart He thinks
There cd be some truth to that statement
He thinks it's a puzzle unfamiliar with it
Consulting the 35c SOLUTIONS and succumbs

The dread cure of unending durable sadness the next
Afternoon when he goes out on the street
Scowling and angry at salesgirls and other

Pleasant people he met on the Washington
March which is just another windy picnic
You expect it to overhaul yr daydream con-
Structions but litter covers the field
The girls show up wearing society bandanas
While the band makes another stab at *Poinciana*
Everybody is dying to hear it And you
Impounded with the ghostlies of Europe
That hung over the armchair like a doily
Protect from greasy honesty and black
Esteem, he sez walking out of the diner
It is because these islands rise in the river
And we think of our blood its sly ambition
And our slavery barges ahead disappear under
This gray cloud the river's facile attention
Gray Cloud looking for his people's genius
In the river which only admits his own face
This is the price one must pay. The world
He looks for with its ragged elevator boys and
Cleaning women and a society as it has schemed
The great buildings fawning over the river
Having outgrown its parents now teach them
The message in eyes. Uh huh and though they fakers
What doctor can be more a charlatan than his patient
Like the people you ask about the movie who answer
Delightful and with a straight face you ask about
His is a masterful face the screen proudly welcomes
Which is our way of presenting constant relations
She coughs mention It is like Electricity, boring.
Everyone think so but they get up each morning
Above the street the trio in the Church watch over
That which they Monday again and struggle with it
Under the white flags of your excuse me pretentiously
Sitting back in her round shouldered chair and her
One hand sending transcriptions of the boredom back
To the small cafeteria where he sits and suffers
Heartburn in a business trip city thinking of her.
Only the caution of his opinions remaining after she
Shut up his mouth Moments and how beautiful she—

The housing project stands out from the dim street like skywriting
Like the Geographic snapshot as the political ones
Stumble into another picturesque valley and portals
An odd religion shaped like a flower, darkening up
Recent progress has given hope to those who had no hope
The project sings its white verses in the pollution
Glad to have the piece of the newspaper PROGRESS
Wait for its husband to arise from the flowering speeches
The air itself speaking You know the enormity of it
The syndicate across in the Cleaners
I even don't dare go out my door
Since the suggestion of the damn shame these hours
Another magazine comes with red black and green cover
She chenile housecoat against the white plaster
Project walls one hand pretend to serve the blues
At the table the mail must comment on it later
Certainly more wanted out of life than life wanted
And she wants a weak man she becomes the need
Of his heart The one we think is strongest
Among us, she pins up in her mirrored desire be-
Cause men wrong about these things the only thing
She ever is sure she correct

Black night is the shape of her man, his face says
The fancy new suit in the lamp appears to say "1940"
Give a possible explanation (a) What is the name
Of the machine assuming gravity the shoulder what
It is to sit on the bottom of a canoe together
And read the diagnosis of the fire as it answers
Their impatient questions with titles of old songs
Bringing back to them the views they have cherished
Her face in the exuberant filmlight The sun-
Or the lace smoke around them, like a picture that
Could never hang near the TV set it wd threaten
Your investment or it inspire sick phone calls and
The new act where like a sleepwalker you come onstage
Monday afternoon when she turns her face to the city
The south side of town disappears,
Sleepwalker! If nothing else shows in the sky we wd

Say her face is an emblem of it and unhappily blame
Arguments on her Rob and demean ourselves in her honor
These streets, bars that jail us in our own static
And punish us with the silly bazaar WHEEL OF FORTUNE
Every number our number and always come up the same

And still beyond the heavy blues we dream is perspiration
He reads in a book of Indian metaphysics and thinks
Gray Cloud, the construction man who walks above our
Vanished fantasy slum and her face in the light the
Projection of these dim photographs he finds himself
Imprisoned are stills from Grade B movies is history
The ragged jungles cardboard drawing rooms mysterious
Mouthwash as on the lawns of the new project
She meets him and give him her Jean Simmons smile
Subway repeat after me the Sioux mirror blam blam
Why don't we go out and steal something someone
Why don't we go out and steal something someone
"You're fired" Why don't you get a job and get
Some religion ambassador Gray Cloud the secret spy
It is amazing what can now be done with reinforced cement
You are one nasty individual "Why Charlie, this is
A surprise!" Black dreamer, this time will you let
That nigger go or will you bury him again with the blues
Fearing his greasy mouth the raucous voice that haunts
The Alhambra   Will he get lost in the shuffle as we
Come back to the room to play whist and laugh about it
Like the old movies in which we cleverly conceal our-
Selves and not so cleverly sniff out another slum ABC
News reports on affluence delinquent Negro History Week
THEY ARE BACK ON THE BLOCK as if it were a song.

The garden is the name of the machine its windows
Return from the sky bringing telegram flowers
As a figure of speech. We are flying up the happy
Thoughts of pebbles, he thinks And she thinks so
Which means it is true and becomes the beautiful
New housing projects where Sunday afternoons they sit
Reading the papers and watching Gray Cloud die again

So they forget the papers think of the lost one
Who thinks of Manhattan and white clouds of sun
From their picture windows darken with our lies
And flying saucers at last come to take you your wife
Runs off with the junkman and left all yr clothes
Still in the laundry but the space in your heart
Is black surrounding white flowers that grow in yr
Heart Wrapped up as a present by the right hand

Your gift frightens you and you throw it away but
It is the monument of the right hand
Stalking from its sophisticate mummification
And chase its futuristic lover in the night
She have packed up and gone to the City
Which answers the white paper with grime
She answers the pleading heart with her
Absence saying that a man do not weep
Without a good reason, that she is not
Here is not reason enough for your tears
Your awful moaning It is worthwhile to say
The slum's gardens receive your sobbing
With the disdain the street imposes on its
Unfortunate and desperate romance with sun
And rain and snow flurries and the emotions
Of people who carelessly mow the lawn
And the flowers people who fill their life
With colorless alarm clocks and murders
To justify the love in their life, lovers
This is something I know. These blues
Will never get more polite and leave us
Friends, put back her comfortable dust-
Cloth These blues will never get lost
We walk the early hours of tomorrow through white
Streets we are afraid to possess   We walk
In the night and bundle our shadows around us
Hiding the part of us that turns white and
Lingers on the quiet streets we go through
The tidy fraud that suggests we are negroes

SECRETS OF THE SAMBA

Part of it thought up in the silence
Of a modernistic hall, the chart
In front of them showing the fake
Limits they discover and accept
Like the silence itself collagiste

Transaction, the unexpected retard
As more breath is drawn magically
Into their mechanical lungs soft
Expressions quitting mechanical lips
Planting new discoveries under seats.

They do not ask which one requested
Thunder breaking outside and rain
Or walk up the dingy steps and leave
Silly notes on her door his door
Discovery nothing, the facts alone

Clear in this manner as other questions
Why are there always those they do not
Feel a shameful curious sting wet breeze
Shall it keep them hidden inside samba
That they know nothing about and refuse

To ask anybody How can you tell
Who knows and could explain it
Is just something else one pretends
Before friends to have discovered

The white beard leads one among scholars
And discovery of what perfectly obvious
Sustains their eyesight in the dim library
What astigmatic mitre corners and crowns
Them these questions they don't even ask

Insist they believe their discoveries
Turn their hair white turn their eye
White put white coats on them and send
Them into libraries and labs asking
Mechanics to fix up the blink in the

Samba the secret samba winking
Like their appreciative and far from
Eloquent neighbors and uncles who
Mean to say you look like a beatnik
The wink light betrays the ragged
Discretion, the silent white coats

MODERN PLUMBING ILLUSTRATED

Fresh andirons trap the working class flat
Suddenly we are in England
Every arch on the boulevard reminds me to be ready for that
School which is marble slab a rock and roll band
Piping amid the sinking projects
Lead reminds me of the highest standards of work. It is fitting
That a fresh connection be made between the padded shoulders
Of the public, the distant verandah.
Later, we are composed by the method known in America as "soil"
We become fixtures on a foreign baseball
Field, planning strategic moves in Aden from third base.
We become indigenous and local, venting calypso foil
We become experts on trombone plungers
Beyond this, everything is watery and confused.
When I lifted the ashtray ashes and sparks
Inspired the classical desk. It has been adopted and abused
Country plumbing by Oral R______* in the Arkansas
Country plumbing crusades contain views
Of lowdown water closets across big red on white mechanical drawings for
Piping amid the stinking projects called in this place
"The liberal Durham system"** he puts his hand on your dick
"Abundant healing life is the answer
Let me hold your hand. You don't really want to marry my sister"
Then we ignore his pious shudders for tropical brain
Fever a blackboy religion of violent coats
We have to say "yeah Newk, pick
The mother fucker off at first, hit the mother fucker make im chaw
His own teeth golly, look at that 'bloody' face"
Newk another triumph for the race.

*Oral Roberts, a pioneer of TV evangelism.
**Type of plumbing characterized by particular kinds of iron / lead etc—definition of it from the book which presumably gives the poem its title, R. M. Starbuck's *Modern Plumbing Illustrated.*

THE SUBWAY WITNESSES

Who are they to be in their skin,
Flags drip off them
And they appear to the mighty
In dreams of white dope.
Pictures of airplanes over
The Manchukuo hunger
Who could have done this to them
Dreams of the mighty and
Cowled hearts of the awesome
Night created now
Of handsome affairs.
Like the head of the young archery
Instructor as it marries
The fiberglass arch of his
Back; it is beautiful
Or terror to expire in tunnels.
Pick one. Ask who are you
To be frightened   who to see
Bloodshed this once and
Not to be blinded, heroic and aimlessly quick
To revenge. Revenge.
Stupid people, don't sit here
This is the throne of the
Mummy   who walks the reeling night
From front to back
Swinging between its thoughts,
Ecstasies of the dry arms
That enfold you as you stiff-
Would be caught in the new
Arms of your bodies that fear the blade
From the naked bookshops and
Stewed theatres of the approaching
Entrance we make into the
Film of our laughing endurance,
Our hands   icepicks and soft blood
Blood in our pockets.

TWO ONE-ACT PLAYS

INTOLERANCE

The audience, once seated in the theater, will become impatient. They will "want something to happen." When the director is of the opinion that the audience is at the crucial point of impatience, that point where the decision is made either to leave or remain, he will begin the play. An actor enters and announces that the performance will be delayed for a specific period of time. His lines are improvised, but the delay he announces must not be either too great or too minor: in the first case, audience anticipation would be destroyed; in the latter, unease and dissatisfaction would find an outlet. The actor exits and five minutes later, regardless of the delay he has announced, one thousand men enter and physically assault the audience.

THE FRENCH REVOLUTION*

The audience, once seated in the theater, will become impatient. They will "want something to happen." When the director is of the opinion that the audience is at the crucial point of impatience, that point where the decision is made either to leave or remain, he will begin the play. An actor enters and announces that the performance will be delayed for a specific period of time. His lines are improvised, but the delay he announces must not be either too great or too minor: in the first case, audience anticipation would be destroyed; in the latter, unease and dissatisfaction would find an outlet. The actor exits and five minutes later, regardless of the delay he has announced, one thousand men enter and physically assault the audience.

*To insure that "The French Revolution" is not confused with "Intolerance," the director must be certain that the costumes are authentic and that tickets for "The French Revolution" are priced at a figure accessible only to a particularly well-to-do class of theater-goers. In staging "Revolution," the director might find it advisable to dispense with the one spoken part and to delay his opening curtains until after the audience has already commenced a disgusted exodus. The cast may then attack them in the lobby (where the usual French Provincial furnishings will be appropriate).

SELENA

Can you read my gestures?
Do you understand my song?

Yes, I outstretch my hand to you
Showing a brand-new quarter
Shiny in my open palm
I'm saying "You are beautiful
And I love you"

My guess,

If I could touch you
You'd be cold but cold
As marble that responds
By capturing the heat of a caress
Making me bold

Ardor and madness

Prompts this song

Disturbed by your serenity
Never knowing where you will appear
This song is improvised
And I am anything except composed

Men with impressive new machines
Claim they can calculate
What distance means—
Graphing the vagility of your flirtations

I only know your silence

How luminous and strange,
You tempt mute resonance

But it's just that aloof encouragement
That makes me sing

FROM THE WORKING DAYS

That other kid took off

He's spent an hour now
            trying to find
A way to fill a shadow
            and look busy, too
Keeping in motion
            looking purposeful
To escape
            getting something hard to do

Staring
            across the bright Mart's
All-night aisles
Admiring the young women
            of poor neighborhoods
Most of whom will never be
            so beautiful again
Most of whom will always be poor
            if they live long enough
            to see gray hair
Believing the haphazard obligatos
            of survival
Must have been choices

(The kind unkind Blues divas
Carved in wax
As cut him if he stand or shoot him
            if he run)

                        Tomorrow
In a lecture hall somewhere
Some other women, much more fortunate
Than those he ogles here
If he should cross their minds

Insist his stare is leaching power
From these girls

Enough
As if that gaze (and something
                in his blood
Between his legs or just between us guys)
Will launch him
Faultlessly as NASA's shuttle
                to an Executive Suite
As surely as his grunting heft
From the far reaches
                of the parking lot
Propels a line of 50 shopping carts
Into the cart corral

A feat of youthful strength
That merits gasps

but don't you know,
                most nights
Not one of these young women
As they glide smiling chatting to & fro
                can see him
But you can bet
Bright as the harvest moon
                he rises into view
For the Night Mgr's assistant nuisance
(Who probably had his job
                3 years ago)

                                soon
As he lights a cigarette
For some cute someone
Or by some awkward miracle
Strikes up a conversation

THE MIDNIGHT SUN

I was a sort of golden lad in California
Collecting barflies
Child voiced but wily blonds,
Desperate red-haired suburban moms
Dancing all night in Country Western bars
Washed up by their daughters' menstrual flow
Shuffling two-step, complex Cotton Eyed Joe

A different sense of warmth each night
Different perfumes, indifferent beds
With sappy songs to prove us human
On the soundtracks in our minds. Dancing
To evict the stubborn gargoyles
Scowling behind sunglasses in the shadows
Of our recollections. A gleaming hero.

Mirrors awake like a stepchild's conspiracies
Spilling angles

Contrived to be two men in one,
I was both the flint and the spark
Your radiance of afternoon
Her maestro of the dark

GOOD HOUSEKEEPING

Nothing in that drawer.
—Ron Padgett

Lost Santa Fe sun catcher
Complete with suction cup and hook
Suddenly discovered in a kitchen drawer

A sepulchre of cooking tools
Useless for a chef
Whose specialty is coffee by the cup

Is caught here, instant clarity
Something just as obsolete
From the same era

Why all our treasured sages
Ranted against the ease
So natural to us, of accumulation

Reminds me why Ra-Meses
Had Luxor completely redone
His name on every stone

The archeology of absent love
Explains our always necessary war on history
A simple act. A saving pride

FIVE EMPTY REAMS

How much sadder
Must the words I choose
Become
Before there is no sadness left
In three dimensions

How much paper will I have to use

MILLENARIAN JOYS

There was a time when quality was stressed
And finite, broke. The brownstones fade.
The year was back in 1999
The "Devil's Somersault"
Was just a kid then, moping on the farm

A jubilee of minor unimportance
My name is whatever you want to call me
And, yes, I am bucolic.
A boldness of robins on hobo
Heading distractedly north
Surrounds me at the door.

Somewhere I think I heard
About a strange secluded people
Content but limited
To trash-and-sleaze economics
A tribe confused with
So much information
They live 24 hours a day

Nothing else happens.

No one comes by
Except the birds. And
They just drop in on the fly
Searching for more
                                        quality time
From fading brownstones
                irises
A field devours the eye

WALKING VICKSBURG BLUES

History is still ephemera
To begin with
Before relics and locks
Corsets and stays
Were fact and stocks
Pillories
That was the truth

I walked along the dark lonely
Road
I walked beside the fields of Dudley Pillow
I walked in Mississippi and Louisiana
And felt the negro terror of a moonless night
Baptized in more history than I wanted

If it's history you're after
Pray we all of us survive each day
That's lease enough. To still the devil's laughter.
Think of it this way:
4 billion simultaneous chest x-rays.

A MINGUS MEMORY

Test test
You don't know what love is
Your
But there is so much
Or craziness
Noise
In the club
Tinkling of glasses
No, he said
Cash register ringing
And the cats
Who was there
Ah hum
Eric Danny Ted Curson
Lonnie Hillyer maybe
Eyes
Everybody sez "huh"
Finally, he shouts
He shouts it out
WHAT LOVE
As, probably, he
Should did in the first place

You don't know you
Are
And you are *not* living
Up to your potential

HOLLANDAISE SALSA

Life, Lord, is beautiful
Ricardo and I wandering around
Find Chili people & the salsa sound
Near Leidseplein

Amazing! We go in and bullshit
                                        Texas-style

Oh yes,

In Amsterdam the streets are colonies
Named for the late empire
Colonised by landlord greed for rent
TE KOOP downtown, round town the rent is steep
And squatters boggling police with signs
On F. Bolstraat
BEZET and portents tell me this is usual business

Ricardo tells me, Don't forget yourself
These people don't like you Vato
They made a fortune off your ancestors
These Dutch

So many streets in Amsterdam
Bear names of colonies
And Amsterdamers are surprised
Terrorism and hate in Holland?

South Moluccans? who in hell is that?
What else did they expect

They named these streets in all their greed of glory
Someone else's pain

At 4 am
A couple Surinam boys sit around Muntplein
And chat
They've nowhere to go, no flat
No blond Dutch girl, no customers for hash
They sit and chat
                                        No dark girl either

Lord
            Life can be like that

And yes,
I walk into tomorrow's obligations
I watch the ducks fret in Sarphatipark
I call for Jessica (of course, she's late)
A black man's jogging
And brown children squeal

I recognize this . . .

Walking this Sunday along Albert Cuyp
The market vanished into square Dutch homes
The Kaseko the Salsa leaking out of windows
Of the lost lost in their Sunday dreaming

I'm home

DIPLOMACY

Tonight, I count my sins
An exercise
The kind of thing
The most unwinnable of games
A solitary state of mind
Devises. Nothing to do
With conscience or contrite
Renunciation

Simply to fill up time
And block ideas
That might just generate
Additional complaints

Nothing is gained, perhaps
Except to understand
The eye-piercing cologne men wear
To transact filthy business

GO TO BED ANYWAY

Knowing I will not sleep tonight,
Counting my blessings and the day's
Obscenities,

Measure what our champions
Have achieved—
A politics of filth and innuendo,
Public discourse degraded into smut
Samson's blind triumph
Pulls down the fortress of the enemy
On our own heads

Knowing I will not sleep tonight,
Tomorrow is a fiction
For those who need a dream

NOWHERE NEAR ALBUQUERQUE

Should have saved money
Now they economize on words
Use just enough to spoil
The vacancy where storms are built

His purposeful departure for the office
Disguises what he knows:

A wandering
That seems to be approaching 40 years
Not all his life,
But all that he can reach

She should have had the sense
To be pretentious
At least they'd have
More trivial problems

At home and twenty feet away
He likes the rattle of her desert bracelets

Her silver hair in Pocahontas braids

AN EDUCATION

Our academy was the 5 Spot's FIRE door
Where Sunny Murray
Soft-spoken Socrates
In frayed blue jeans
The essence of the Blues
No love, he says, no money
His own music too strange
Even for jam sessions in the afternoon
Amid a traffic jam of spirits
Interpreted the flames of beauty
Rushing through the door
Mingus searing
So caliente in the house
Izzy always left that door ajar
Blue corona of Ted Curson's horn
Sinuous pharaonic bass clarinet
Shouting out Eric's alarm
Octave above octave
Beneath the rumbling earthquake
Dannie Richmond's drums
And bells of Jaki Byard

Light-bending summer heat outdoors
The smoldering blue room
Once a month I had enough
To pay the cover charge;
But the music was never so sweet
As those hot nights
When we eavesdropped
As genius told the spirits like it is
Just how we humans feel

DOWNTOWN BOOM

There are no gospel singers
Anymore

On the corners
They held down for Jesus
Valets park cars
At restaurants for fancy people
On expense accts or dates

So many times
People come up to me
And say, Billy
Hey wait a minute
You not Billy!

You can see the new ballpark
Just past the courthouse

But which way is redemption?

AILERONS & ELEVATORS

Autumnal Equinox 2002

The backward see
The wise don't say a word

Three dreams, one foolish
And two meaningless
Are haunting me, disturbing me

One says
A golden road was plotted out for you
In dreams, of course

But that's not where you are
When you awaken

The danger is seeing the world
    as two extremes
The afternoons of rushing home to see her
Balanced against
    turning the corner
Hoping that her car will not be there

Daydreams are better

Nice—
watching the planes come in
On the last day of summer
Airport peaceful

Passengers are few
On flights answering demand
      more than desire
Their stress has been at home
Or will come later

They deplane calmly

When the Wright boys
    and their friend Paul Laurence Dunbar
Finished high school   in 1890
Their neighbors knew
That they'd go high up in this world
Paul as an elevator boy in downtown Dayton
Orville and Wilbur
Going swimming in thin air

Unfortunately,
They'd never heard
    of Richard Gallup
David *or* Romare Bearden, either

Such are the baffling deficits that time imposes

They never dreamed
Someone would use an airplane
To drop bombs made of oilfield dynamite
    and set Greenwood aflame
Andrew Smitherman fleeing   in 1921
    from Tulsa to New York
To the edge of America

What is this shadow
Cast across the coming season?

In the still watches of the Negro night,
Fear rising like mist off a bayou,
The danger in the world
Is seeing it as two extremes

Is this full moon so indiscriminate
That even liars prosper
    if they have launched
Their web with the new moon?

This autumn equinox
A harvest of deceit
Leaves the ground rugged.
The harvest done, the fields outside the city
    flat and sere
A single egret
    stands in the parking lot at the Post Office
Poised and confused

The world automatically recoils
Into itself

Are you ready for football?
For serious business
Are you ready for *war*?

People throughout all history
Have lived in ashen cities
or died in them
Marcel Duchamp was joking
Wasn't he, as always
    When he said
Dust covered glass
Might offer auguries
Of our predicament

O mirror, mirror

How have my people been distracted so
They don't care any longer who they are?

How so misled that they believe
Punishment does not apply
To crimes committed in their name?

Must war morph from Nintendo game to spectacle
To get attention?

If all are suspect
Could my own duplicities
Be causing this—
The way we're all responsible
For air pollution

(if you keep breathing

If you believe in magic, yes

And that same magic, yes
Could stop the rush to madness, too

There are still
    scraps of summer laughter
On the street
There's still some music
    from two backyards away
The Funkadelics and Jay-Z resist denial

But here's
The truth:

You have the right to keep your mouth shut

Trust me,

Across the room
A person looking like a crazy version
    Of somebody you once knew
Might be our Savior
One who can draw fire
    Out of ashes
At least a lover, maybe
The one to take you up a little higher
    Or let you down easy.

But don't look this way,

It isn't me

AN ARC STILL OPEN

I

Words, like all splendid things
Familiar or obscure
Can tarnish over time
Telling a story is a burnishing
Smoothing & polishing the syllables
To bright reflection

We call that memory

The ancients said,
losing an elder
Is to lose a library

Then they invented Art
To stem such loss

We are men of woman born
And human being
Singers we are, and makers
Aspiring towards manhood, womanhood
A sanity of spirit known as grace

We thrive on mysteries
What can be made with fire and water
Wood and stone
Carefully selected mud
Work authorizes shapeliness
But vision creates form

II

When care and kindness
Compassion and concern
Direct the mind
The motion of the intellect becomes a dance
And the deft hand
Can speak
Can weave or work sacred geometries
That section space into the arcs
Of humane understanding
And joyous trace of song

The watcher then becomes
The seer and the doer

The wall records the hand's reach
As the hand records the mind's

That was the way he took
That was John's path:

Griot, storyteller
Soft-spoken but loquacious sage
Alchemist of words and images
Child of Anancy, spinner of magic phrase

Sometimes this world of entropy and haste
Seems nothing more than a vast depot
With everyone of us,
Stressed, nonchalant,
Traveling light or heavy burdened
In passage—
Chasing the tortoise and the hare
In endless round

III

Treasure our moments and our meetings here
Treasure the story and the memory
That will remain to testify when we embark
Upon the next stage of our neverending journey

Statements

Statement for *Jambalaya: Four Poets*

(Reed, Cannon and Johnson, 1975)

I consider myself to be a student of Aural Design, a practitioner of Sound Science. My poetry is drawn from the oral tradition of Black peoples as well as the literary traditions of the West (most of which are based on Black or Oriental origins). Aesop is the eponymous Ethiopian and Homer is simply Omar mispronounced by thin Grecian lips. Poetry is an instrument that we study in order to free the spirit, to celebrate the ancestors. My writing is based upon the discipline of Sound Science, which is necessary when we now have people who can play "Rhapsody in Blue" on a Marine Band harp; of course there were some who could play that before George Gershwin. See what I mean? One of the main elements of my work is volume adjustment and another is reality transformation. Which are ways of saying that Black Art's purpose is to provide SPACE for living and growth. I believe we need it. I give all praises to the Creator and dedicate all my effort toward a better world.

Statement for the anthology *None of the Above*

(Crossing Press, 1976)

Poetry is a spiritual, social & political revelation. A force. An effort to welcome a better world. I see things & write them down & call it poetry, though they used to teach us this was "fantasy." It's not. I see things so often, my mind suggests words. I think about the words for several days until I decide to write something. Then I take several sheets of typing paper, fold them in half into a little book & scribble on it. My thoughts & notes are jotted down in bits & pieces just as I think. Later, I read & revise it; alphabetize & number each distinct section. Just like in a warehouse. The final step involves juggling the sections around & typing them in a revised sequence. That's the poem, story or essay. It's like mixing & editing magnetic tape. I'm trying to get better at writing the bits down so that others reading/hearing these words can see what it was I thought I saw. These are the ingredients. Or, concerns: 1) Every church (or secular 'temple' or edifice) is an artifice built upon a particular natural thing (a cave, a spring, a network of oil wells, discount stores, etc.) which someone has attached to a spiritual or social idea. Like poems, all of that is here on planet Earth to be analyzed. All of it, existing, aids to learning one thing. Or another thing. 2) My poetry is about ancient African myths, flowers, Texas, communism, the negro Democratic Club on New York Blvd., taxes, & watching TV. Several women who are more real than ideas or poems. Does that sound like a Country & Western tune? Drinking beer. 3) My poetry is more urban than rural & is connected with the experience of the masked media as an accepted "natural" element of life. Its purpose (technique, if I'm doing it right) is a critical analysis of that worldview which makes *TV Guide* the most widely circulated periodical in the modern world as we know it. In that sense, the poems are at once personal & political. 4) I am serious about what I do. Even sullen. The problem with satirists is that they are always too quick to recognize notions dictated by folly. 5) No. Actually, these are all poems of love & lust. Or religious poems. Verse. Witchcraft. Songs. Cartoons. Epithalamia. Toasts, boasts. Dissertations about ranking lies. Which is the same thing.

Although you don't see crazy niggers & white kids on TV anymore talking about Revolution, don't be fooled &/or dismayed. We will have us a better world. Here. And soon. I came to this country speaking Spanish. In school, I fooled around with English, German, & French. The next time I left, I was speaking broken Vietnamese.

This is a recipe for the salsa that will baste the future (if I am remembering what the old people taught me aright.) Stir it up.

List:
I enjoy reading the works of the following writers because they provide their readers with a revolutionary vortex in terms of opening one's eyes to a larger social & spiritual reality: Joan Bergier & Louis Pauwels, Christopher Caudwell, Joseph Goodavage, Lawson Fusao Inada, Joe Johnson, Hazrat Inyat Khan, Gerald Massey, Ezekiel Mphalele, Simon Ortiz, Tran Te Xuong. I can understand it if you haven't heard of some of these people. But you will.

Introduction to *Chances Are Few*

(second edition: Blue Wind Press, 2003)

What poetry is exactly about, or what it's for, has never actually occupied too much of my thinking. I have assumed the answer to those questions has always been "anything" and "everything." Poetic license simply amounts to what the old people in New Orleans say when babies cry: "Sure you right, darling, let them know you here!"

Some people would have poetry limit itself to pleasing the quick-witted mind; others, to exploring the ever-fearful soul. Some would permit those activities as long as artists also help us confront large social issues. A good job for whoever is brave enough to have it.

This modern world—what T. S. Eliot taught us to call "our civilization"—began in 1492 with a series of cultural collisions that continue to reverberate. We've had five hundred grim years of progress: a kaleidoscope of ancient fears and hatreds, bright visions and hopeful dreams, justifiable suspicions and ordinary greed, constantly recycled as history becomes everyday life and vice versa.

Now that's something to talk about. But I never felt comfortable telling anyone that I dreamed of a grand purpose for my poems. I didn't go out looking to write poems. Poems simply appeared when it was necessary to write them; when something happened to me—physically, emotionally, perhaps spiritually—that demanded that I have something to say.

I found myself wandering around in America, looking at what there was to be looked at, following some path determined by curiosity and chance—the x and y of human being. Maybe it was just the restlessness of youth? Youth is devoted to adventure but aspires to knowledge. Usually, of course, all one gets is experience.

Always, it has seemed sensible to me to accept the proposition that the poet is the man who suffers; that to speak of that suffering helps us to understand how such experiences shape people and the world. Understanding such things might teach us how to make life less painful, our relationships less brutal. As our nightly entertainments and the watchman's alarums both reveal, ours is a society full of brutalities decked out in excuses. True civility would show us how to install intelligence and wisdom in the place now haughtily occupied by destructive sophistication.

Wisdom, according to the proverbs of Solomon, "crieth at the gates, at the entry of the city." Question is, who listens? Writing poems involves that desperate attempt to pass through sophistication into wisdom. So the poet—disdaining fashion—tries on hats and costumes, modes and forms. Takes soundings. There is always the need to find and recognize beauty. Wherever we are. And, as Ricardo Miro insists, there is the need to tell the truth.

Looking again at the poems in *Chances Are Few*—a title that pays homage to the hypnotically beautiful gospel-tinged acetylene blues of Baby Face Willette—I believe that what is said here is at least honest. And, I think, mostly true.

Anyway, as Ned Sparks puts it in the original *Imitation of Life*, "That's my story and I'm sticking to it."

ACKNOWLEDGMENTS

Fit Music

Acknowledgment note that appeared in original 1972 edition of *Fit Music* and again when the poem "Fit Music" was republished in *The Bathers* in 1981:

"Several lines in sections V and VIII are quoted from Ezra Pound, *The Classic Anthology Defined by Confucius* (Cambridge: Harvard University Press, 1954), and from "Little Honda" by Brian Wilson (Sea of Tunes Publishing Company, BMI); and a few lines in "Envoy" paraphrase "Is It Yes Or Is It No" by James Brown (King Music, BMI). Acknowledgment is made to these poets for their timelessness and aptness of thought. — L.T."

All poems by Lorenzo Thomas reprinted by permission of the Literary Executors for Lorenzo Thomas.

Where poems were collected in books, they are here presented as in their book appearance. Those books were:

Fit Music (New York: Angel Hair Books, 1972).
Dracula (New York: Angel Hair Books, 1973).
Jambalaya: Four Poets, (New York: Reed, Cannon and Johnson, 1975).
Framing the Sunrise (Houston: Sun Be/Am Associates, 1975).
Sound Science (Houston: Sun Be/Am Associates, 1978).
Chances Are Few (Berkeley: Blue Wind Press, 1979, revised 2003).
The Bathers (New York: I. Reed Books, 1981).

The works appearing under "Additional Poems" have not previously appeared in larger collections.

The black and white drawings from *Fit Music* are reproduced by permission of the artist, Cecilio Thomas.

As always, we thank the editors and publishers of Lorenzo Thomas's works for their support over the years.

We particularly thank Karen Luik for her dedication to Lorenzo Thomas in his life and beyond. Anne Waldman, who was among the first to publish Thomas, and Ted Greenwald, a friend of Thomas's from his teenage years to his passing, both have given great encouragement to this project. Suzanna Tamminen and her colleagues at Wesleyan University Press have been not only utterly professional, but also enthusiastic about this work from the first tentative inquiry through to publication. David Grundy and Jean-Philippe Marcoux gave valuable assistance in tracking down stray poems. Anna Everett was one of those remarkable friends who tended to gather around Lorenzo Thomas, and she spent memorable Boulder July Fourths with him and Harryette Mullen and others. She has, from the outset, been a loving supporter of this collection and its collectors. Aldon Nielsen hereby records his ever-mounting debt of gratitude to her and adds a note of respect and admiration for Laura Vrana. Laura Vrana, in her turn, adds "I am indebted to my supportive partner Matt, to my indefatigable coeditor, and to Lorenzo Thomas for this richly inspiring work."

Finally, the occasionally fatigued coeditors wish to thank that nearly mythical being, the contemporary poetry reader, on behalf of the ever-gracious Lorenzo Thomas.

INDEX OF TITLES

INDEX OF FIRST LINES

About the Author

LORENZO THOMAS was born in the Republic of Panama in 1944 and emigrated with his family to New York in 1948. In New York, he was a part of the Black Arts Movement and was one of the youngest members of the Umbra Workshop, a landmark group for emerging black poets. After naval service in Vietnam (1968–72), Thomas moved to Houston, Texas, and was a writer-in-residence at Texas Southern University. From 1984 until his death in 2005, he was a professor of English at the University of Houston–Downtown.

About the Editors

ALDON LYNN NIELSEN was the first winner of the Larry Neal Award for poetry, and has appeared in both *The Best American Poetry* and *Best American Experimental Writing*. His most recent volume of poetry is *You Didn't Hear This from Me*. His works of scholarship include *Black Chant* and *Integral Music*. Nielsen is the George and Barbara Kelly Professor of American Literature at the Pennsylvania State University, and also teaches at Central China Normal University. With Cecilio Thomas, he serves as Literary Executor for Lorenzo Thomas.

LAURA VRANA is an assistant professor of English, specializing in African American literature and poetry, at the University of South Alabama. Her work has appeared in the journals *Obsidian: Literature & Arts in the African Diaspora* and *Journal of Ethnic American Literature*.